Contents

Italian Broccoli Rabe Grinder	5
Italian Rice Croquettes	5
Bren's Italian Meatballs	7
Italian Veggie Rolls	7
Make-Ahead Manicotti	8
Italian Beef For Sandwiches	9
Slow Cooker Italian Beef	10
Cioccolata Calda (Hot Chocolate Italian-Style)	10
Homemade Italian Cream Soda	11
Italian Amaretto Margaritas On The Rocks	11
Easy Italian Sausage And Rigatoni	12
Manicotti Italian Casserole	13
Italian Onion Cucumber Salad	14
Aunt Rita's Italian Stew	14
Quick Bean And Turkey Italian Meatballs	15
Italian Nutthouse Broiled Tomatoes	16
New York Italian Style Cheesecake	16
Italian Cheesecake	17
Italian Style Brunch Cakes	18
Creamy Italian Dressing Ii	19
Italian Tomato Cucumber Salad	19
Italian-Style Pork Tenderloin	20
Italian Turkey Zoodles	21
Italian Wedding Cookies	23
Slow Cooker Italian Beef For Sandwiches	23
Italian Gravy	24
Italian Sauce	25
Italian Enchiladas	26
Italian Tacos	26
Italian Peas	27
Italian Kale	28
Italian Wedding Soup	28
Italian Rib Eye	29
Italian Cookies Ii	30
Johnsonville Italian Meatballs	30
Old Italian Meat Sauce	31

- Southern Italian Thanksgiving Stuffing ... 32
- Quick Italian Skillet Dinner ... 33
- Italian Stuffed Chicken Breast ... 34
- Italian Pasta Salad I ... 35
- Special Italian Easter Pizza ... 36
- Quick Italian Vegetable Soup ... 37
- Italian Halibut Chowder ... 38
- Bowties And Italian Sausage ... 39
- Italian Stewed Tomatoes ... 40
- Italian Nachos Restaurant-Style ... 40
- Italian Sausage - Tuscan Style ... 41
- Italian-Style Strawberry Shortcake ... 42
- Italian Sausage And Bean Soup ... 42
- Granny's Italian Zucchini Pie ... 43
- Italian Spaghetti Squash ... 44
- Simple Italian Omelet ... 45
- Italian Butterball Cookies ... 46
- Italian Fig Cookies Ii ... 46
- Aunt Rita's Italian Stew ... 48
- Potato Soup Italian Style ... 48
- Italian-Style Bruschetta ... 49
- Alligator Animal Italian Bread ... 50
- Italian Cream Soda ... 51
- Italian Shrimp Caprese Pasta ... 51
- Spinach Manicotti With Italian Sausage ... 52
- My Best Chicken Piccata ... 53
- Italian Sausage Tortellini Soup ... 54
- Best Italian Sausage Soup ... 55
- Italian Sausage Soup ... 56
- Manicotti Italian Casserole ... 57
- Italian Meatballs ... 57
- Baked Penne With Italian Sausage ... 59
- Italian Popcorn With Parmesan ... 59
- Italian Vegetable Soup ... 60
- Italian Herb Bread ... 61
- Hot Italian Giardiniera ... 62
- Italian Spaghetti Sauce With Meatballs ... 63

Italian Sausage Soup	64
Italian Pork Tenderloin	65
Creamy Italian Dressing	65
Italian Cream Cake Ii	66
Italian Grilled Cheese Sandwiches	67
California Italian Wedding Soup	68
Italian Subs - Restaurant Style	69
Italian Creme Layer Cake	69
Hearty Italian Meatball Soup	71
Tender Italian Baked Chicken	71
Italian Wedding Cake	72
Mexi-Italian Salsa	73
Chocolate Italian Cream Cake	74
Spicy Italian Salad	75
Sweet Italian Green Beans	76
Italian Pasta Veggie Salad	77
Italian Sausage And Gnocchi Soup	77
Italian Wedding Cookies Ii	78
Nenni's Italian Pork Sausage	79
Italian Bbq Pork Chops	80
Homemade Italian Red Sauce	81
Italian Rice Pie I	81
Ricotta Pie (Old Italian Recipe)	82
Italian Rice Pie Ii	83
Easter Grain Pie	84
Best Italian Sausage Soup	85
Pizzelle-Italian Tradition	86
Creamy Italian Chicken	87
The Italian Irishman's Pie	88
Italian Turkey Meatballs	89
Italian Cream Cake	90
Italian Style Turkey Meatloaf	91
Italian Seasoning	91
Italian Style Sausage	92
Italian Sausage And Zucchini	93
Italian Chicken Marinade	93
Party Italian Wedding Soup	94

Italian Lemon Cream Cake 95
Italian Beef Sandwiches 96
Spicy Italian Pork Cutlets 97
Quick Italian Pasta Salad 97
Pasta Sauce With Italian Sausage 98
Three Animal Italian Meatballs 99
Jenni's Italian Farro Pilaf 100
Fuzzy Italian Navel 101
Savory Italian Sausage Sauce 101
Italian Style Pot Roast 102
Italian Sausage Stuffed Shells 103
Italian Meat Sauce I 104
Italian Cabbage Salad 105
Italian Sausage Spaghetti Squash 106
Chunky Italian Spaghetti Sauce 107
Tarradls (Italian Pepper Rings) 107
Italian Style Chili 108
Italian Amaretto Margaritas 109
Italian Onion Cucumber Salad 110
Italian Meat Sauce Ii 110
Beefy Italian Ramen Skillet 111
Baked Italian Lemon Chicken 112
Italian Tuna Spread 113
Prosciutto E Melone (Italian Ham And Melon) 114
Grilled Italian Pork Chops 114
Italian Mini Meat Loaves 115
Italian Meat And Spinach Pie 116
Italian Sausage Penne 117
Italian Lemon Cream Cake 118
Italian Lasagna 119

ITALIAN BROCCOLI RABE GRINDER

Prep: 15 mins - **Cook:** 20 mins - **Total:** 35 mins   - **Servings:** 4

INGREDIENTS

- ½ cup extra-virgin olive oil
- 5 cloves garlic, minced
- 1 teaspoon crushed red pepper flakes
- ½ cup diced pepperoni
- 2 bunches broccoli rabe, trimmed
- 1 pinch salt, to taste
- 4 roll (3-1/2" dia)s hard Italian rolls, split
- 8 slices provolone cheese

DIRECTIONS

Step 1

Heat olive oil in a deep saucepan over medium heat. Stir garlic into the oil; cook and stir until softened but not browned, about 1 minute. Add the crushed red pepper and pepperoni; cook and stir to blend flavors, about 1 additional minute.

Step 2

Stir in the broccoli rabe, coating the leaves well with oil. Cover and cook until broccoli rabe is fully wilted and soft, about 15 minutes. Season with salt.

Step 3

Place a piece of cheese on cut side of each roll; fill with the broccoli rabe mixture. Serve warm.

Cook's Notes

Soak the broccoli rabe in clean, cold water before cooking to be sure to remove any grit.

The key to cooking these is they need to be tender, (like cooked spinach) simmering covered until tender is the key once they've reduced in size.

Nutrition Facts

799.5 calories; protein 30.9g 62% DV; carbohydrates 38.3g 12% DV; fat 58.2g 90% DV; cholesterol 68.9mg 23% DV; sodium 1310mg 52% DV.

ITALIAN RICE CROQUETTES

Prep: 50 mins - **Cook:** 50 mins - **Total:** 1 hr 40 mins - **Servings:** 40

INGREDIENTS

- 2 pounds chicken giblets
- 1 cup water

- ½ teaspoon salt
- 4 cups salted water
- 2 cups long grain white rice, uncooked
- 2 cups grated Parmesan cheese
- ½ cup marinara sauce
- ¼ cup dry bread crumbs
- 2 large eggs large eggs
- 2 tablespoons chopped fresh parsley
- 1 pinch salt and freshly ground black pepper to taste
- 1 cup dry bread crumbs for coating
- 2 cups vegetable oil for frying

DIRECTIONS

Step 1
Combine chicken giblets, 1 cup water, and 1/2 teaspoon salt in a pressure cooker; cook for about 20 minutes.

Step 2
Drain giblets and let cool, about 10 minutes. Chop giblets in a food processor or by hand; set aside.

Step 3
Bring rice and water to a boil in a saucepan over high heat. Reduce heat to medium-low, cover, and simmer until the rice is tender, and the liquid has been absorbed, 20 to 25 minutes.

Step 4
Spread cooked rice onto a baking sheet to cool, about 5 minutes. Transfer rice to a large bowl.

Step 5
Mix in giblets, grated Parmesan cheese, marinara sauce, 1/4 cup bread crumbs, eggs, parsley, salt, and ground pepper. Cover with plastic wrap and refrigerate for 1 hour.

Step 6
Remove rice and giblet mixture from refrigerator and form 2-inch, football shaped croquettes. Roll croquettes in bread crumbs and place on a baking sheet.

Step 7
Heat oil in a large skillet over medium-high heat; cook breaded croquettes until browned on all sides, about 10 minutes. Transfer to a plate lined with paper towels to absorb excess oil.

Cook's Note:

Instead of using pressure cooker, you can simmer the giblets in a saucepan until tender.

Nutrition Facts
99 calories; protein 6.9g 14% DV; carbohydrates 10.4g 3% DV; fat 3.2g 5% DV; cholesterol 60.1mg 20% DV; sodium 139.8mg 6% DV.

BREN'S ITALIAN MEATBALLS

Prep: 15 mins - **Cook:** 15 mins - **Total:** 30 mins - **Servings:** 5

INGREDIENTS

- ½ cup fresh bread crumbs
- ½ cup grated pecorino Romano cheese
- 2 large cloves garlic, minced
- 1 tablespoon chopped fresh parsley
- ¼ teaspoon ground black pepper
- 1 pinch red chili pepper flakes
- 1 egg
- 1 pound lean ground beef

DIRECTIONS

Step 1

Preheat oven to 350 degrees F (175 degrees C). Line a baking sheet with parchment paper.

Step 2

Toss bread crumbs, Romano cheese, garlic, parsley, black pepper, red pepper, and egg together in a bowl; mix in beef gently with your hands. Form beef mixture into meatballs roughly 1 1/4 inches in diameter; place on the prepared baking sheet.

Step 3

Bake in the preheated oven for 10 minutes; turn meatballs and bake until no longer pink at the center, about 5 minutes more. An instant-read thermometer inserted into the center should read at least 160 degrees F (70 degrees C).

Nutrition Facts

258.2 calories; protein 21.8g 44% DV; carbohydrates 3.6g 1% DV; fat 16.8g 26% DV; cholesterol 102.6mg 34% DV; sodium 226.3mg 9% DV.

ITALIAN VEGGIE ROLLS

Prep: 1 hr - **Cook:** 45 mins - **Total:** 1 hr 45 mins - **Servings:** 5

INGREDIENTS

- 1 cup chopped mushrooms
- 1 onion, chopped
- 1 cup sliced carrots
- 1 cup green peas
- 1 cup chopped broccoli

- 1 clove garlic, minced
- ¼ cup dry red wine
- 2 cups shredded mozzarella cheese
- 1 egg
- 2 tablespoons olive oil
- ¼ cup grated Parmesan cheese
- 1 (16 ounce) package lasagna noodles
- 1 (26 ounce) jar spaghetti sauce

DIRECTIONS

Step 1

Cook noodles in a large pot of boiling water until al dente. Rinse, drain, set aside.

Step 2

Heat oil in a medium saute pan. Add mushrooms, onions, carrots, peas, and broccoli; saute over medium heat until tender. Add wine and garlic; cook five minutes, or until wine has just about evaporated. Remove from heat, and cool for ten minutes.

Step 3

In a medium bowl combine sauteed vegetable mixture, mozzarella cheese, 2 tablespoons Parmesan cheese, and egg. Mix well.

Step 4

Pour half of the sauce into the bottom of a 13x9x2inch baking pan. Spread 1/3 cup vegetable mixture over each lasagna noodle then carefully roll up the noodle. Place seam side down in dish. When finished placing all the noodles in the pan, pour remaining pasta sauce evenly over noodles. Cover with aluminum foil.

Step 5

Bake at 375 degrees F (190 degrees C) for 35 to 40 minutes. Uncover, and sprinkle remaining Parmesan cheese over noodles. Bake, uncovered, 5 more minutes. Garnish and serve immediately.

Nutrition Facts

723.4 calories; protein 30.2g 61% DV; carbohydrates 97.1g 31% DV; fat 23.8g 37% DV; cholesterol 79mg 26% DV; sodium 1016.4mg 41% DV.

MAKE-AHEAD MANICOTTI

Prep: 30 mins - **Cook:** 1 hr - **Total:** 1 hr 30 mins - **Servings:** 6

INGREDIENTS

- 1 pint ricotta cheese
- 2 large eggs eggs
- 1 (10 ounce) package frozen chopped spinach, thawed and drained
- 1 cup shredded mozzarella cheese

- ½ cup grated Parmesan cheese
- 1 ½ tablespoons white sugar
- ⅛ teaspoon salt
- ¼ teaspoon ground black pepper
- 12 piece (blank)s manicotti shells
- 1 (32 ounce) jar spaghetti sauce

DIRECTIONS

Step 1

In a medium bowl, mix together ricotta cheese and eggs until blended. Stir in spinach, mozzarella cheese, 1/4 cup of the Parmesan cheese, sugar, salt and pepper. Stuff mixture into uncooked pasta shells.

Step 2

Spread 1/2 cup spaghetti sauce in the bottom of a medium baking dish. Arrange stuffed pasta shells in a single layer over the sauce. Pour the remainder of the sauce over the shells, cover dish, and chill in the refrigerator for 8 hours, or overnight.

Step 3

Preheat oven to 400 degrees F (200 degrees C). Bake covered for 40 minutes. Sprinkle with remaining Parmesan cheese, and bake for another 15 minutes.

Nutrition Facts

506.6 calories; protein 28.8g 58% DV; carbohydrates 55.8g 18% DV; fat 19.1g 29% DV; cholesterol 112.3mg 37% DV; sodium 1057.8mg 42% DV.

ITALIAN BEEF FOR SANDWICHES

Prep: 5 mins - **Cook:** 9 hrs - **Total:** 9 hrs 5 mins - **Servings:** 12

INGREDIENTS

- 1 (4 pound) rump roast
- 1 (12 ounce) jar pepperoncini

DIRECTIONS

Step 1

Place rump roast in a slow cooker, fat-side up. Pour pepperoncini and juice over roast.

Step 2

Cook on Low for 8 hours. Remove fat from roast and shred roast with 2 forks. Simmer roast in the juice for 1 hour more. Remove beef with a slotted spoon.

Cook's Notes:

Depending on taste, may slice the pepperoncinis and serve on the sandwich. Also delicious served with a slice of provolone cheese.

Nutrition Facts

Per Serving:

212.8 calories; protein 26.4g 53% DV; carbohydrates 0.9g; fat 10.7g 16% DV; cholesterol 66.9mg 22% DV; sodium 647.2mg 26% DV.

SLOW COOKER ITALIAN BEEF

Prep: 5 mins - **Cook:** 1 hr - **Total:** 1 hr 5 mins - **Servings:** 6

INGREDIENTS

- 1 pound thinly sliced roast beef
- 1 (.7 ounce) package dry Italian-style salad dressing mix
- 1 (16 ounce) jar pepperoncini, sliced
- 1 (10.5 ounce) can beef broth

DIRECTIONS

Step 1

Combine roast beef, dry dressing mix, pepperoncini, and beef broth in a slow cooker. Cook over medium-high heat until hot, about 1 hour.

Nutrition Facts

113.3 calories; protein 16.5g 33% DV; carbohydrates 5.2g 2% DV; fat 2.8g 4% DV; cholesterol 36.4mg 12% DV; sodium 3033mg 121% DV.

CIOCCOLATA CALDA (HOT CHOCOLATE ITALIAN-STYLE)

Prep: 5 mins - **Cook:** 15 mins - **Total:** 20 mins

INGREDIENTS

- 3 tablespoons cocoa powder
- 1 ½ tablespoons white sugar
- 1 ½ cups milk
- 2 tablespoons milk
- 1 tablespoon cornstarch

DIRECTIONS

Step 1

Mix the cocoa powder and sugar together in a small saucepan. Stir the 1 1/2 cups milk into the saucepan until the sugar has dissolved. Place over low heat; slowly bring the mixture to a low simmer.

Step 2

Whisk 2 tablespoons of milk together with the cornstarch in a small cup; slowly whisk the cornstarch slurry into the cocoa mixture. Continue cooking, whisking continually, until the hot chocolate reaches a pudding-like thickness, 2 to 3 minutes.

Nutrition Facts

169.2 calories; protein 8.1g 16% DV; carbohydrates 26.7g 9% DV; fat 5g 8% DV; cholesterol 15.9mg 5% DV; sodium 83.3mg 3% DV.

HOMEMADE ITALIAN CREAM SODA

Prep: 5 mins - **Total:** 5 mins - **Servings:** 2

INGREDIENTS

- 10 ounces club soda
- 4 ounces heavy cream
- 4 fluid ounces raspberry syrup
- 2 cups ice cubes, or as needed

DIRECTIONS

Step 1

Stir together club soda, heavy cream, and raspberry syrup in a pitcher. Fill 2 tall glasses with ice and pour cream mixture on top.

Cook's Note:

I have made this recipe for 30 people. It can all be mixed in a punch bowl and people will be coming back for seconds, thirds, and fourths!!

Nutrition Facts

416.2 calories; protein 1.2g 2% DV; carbohydrates 56.7g 18% DV; fat 21g 32% DV; cholesterol 77.8mg 26% DV; sodium 27.4mg 1% DV.

ITALIAN AMARETTO MARGARITAS ON THE ROCKS

Prep: 5 mins - **Total:** 5 mins - **Servings:** 4

INGREDIENTS

- 2 tablespoons confectioners' sugar
- 4 cups crushed ice
- 2 cups sweet and sour mix
- 5 fluid ounces tequila
- 5 fluid ounces amaretto (almond-flavored liqueur)
- 2 fluid ounces orange liqueur

- 4 slice (1/4" thick) (blank)s orange slices for garnish
- 4 slice (1/4" thick) (blank)s lime slices for garnish

DIRECTIONS

Step 1

Slightly moisten rims of 4 12-ounce glasses and dip in confectioners' sugar to rim the glasses; fill each with crushed ice.

Step 2

Combine the sweet and sour mix, tequila, amaretto, and orange liqueur in a pitcher; stir. Pour mixture into the prepared glasses. Garnish each drink with orange and lime slices.

Nutrition Facts

539.3 calories; protein 0.2g; carbohydrates 78.7g 26% DV; fat 0.2g; cholesterolmg; sodium 8.4mg.

EASY ITALIAN SAUSAGE AND RIGATONI

Prep: 10 mins - **Cook:** 1 hr 15 mins - **Total:** 1 hr 25 mins - **Servings:** 6

INGREDIENTS

- 1 (8 ounce) package rigatoni pasta
- 1 pound bulk Italian sausage
- ¼ cup diced onion
- 4 cups spaghetti sauce
- 2 cups cottage cheese
- 2 cups mozzarella cheese, divided
- ¼ cup freshly grated Parmesan cheese
- 2 large eggs, beaten
- 1 tablespoon dried parsley
- ½ teaspoon Italian seasoning
- ½ teaspoon dried basil
- 1 pinch salt and ground black pepper to taste

DIRECTIONS

Step 1

Bring a large pot of lightly salted water to a boil. Cook rigatoni in the boiling water, stirring occasionally until tender yet firm to the bite, about 12 minutes. Drain and set aside.

Step 2

Meanwhile, preheat the oven to 350 degrees F (175 degrees C). Grease a large baking dish.

Step 3

Cook sausage and onion in a large skillet until meat is no longer pink and onions are translucent, 5 to 7

minutes.
Step 4
Combine spaghetti sauce, cottage cheese, 1 cup mozzarella cheese, Parmesan cheese, eggs, parsley, Italian seasoning, basil, salt, and pepper in a large bowl. Add sausage and onion mixture; stir until well combined. Add pasta and carefully mix until well incorporated. Transfer to the prepared baking dish and cover.
Step 5
Bake in the preheated oven for 45 minutes. Remove from the oven, top with remaining mozzarella, and bake, uncovered, until cheese is melted, about 15 minutes.

Cook's Note:

Use store-bought or homemade spaghetti sauce. If dish seems too dry, add an additional 1/2 cup spaghetti sauce.

Nutrition Facts
673.3 calories; protein 39.9g 80% DV; carbohydrates 56.5g 18% DV; fat 31.6g 49% DV; cholesterol 133.4mg 45% DV; sodium 1953.3mg 78% DV.

MANICOTTI ITALIAN CASSEROLE

Prep: 10 mins - **Cook:** 30 mins - **Total:** 40 mins - **Servings:** 8

INGREDIENTS
- 1 pound rigatoni pasta
- 1 pound ground beef
- 1 pound Italian sausage
- 1 (8 ounce) can mushrooms, drained
- 2 (32 ounce) jars spaghetti sauce
- 1 ½ pounds shredded mozzarella cheese
- 1 (3 ounce) package thinly sliced pepperoni

DIRECTIONS
Step 1
Preheat oven to 350 degrees F (175 degrees C).
Step 2
Bring a large pot of lightly salted water to boil. Pour in rigatoni, and cook until al dente, about 8 to 10 minutes. Drain, and set pasta aside.
Step 3
Meanwhile, brown ground beef and italian sausage in a large skillet over medium heat. With a slotted spoon, remove beef and sausage to a baking dish. Stir mushrooms, spaghetti sauce, and cooked pasta into the baking dish. Sprinkle cheese and pepperoni over the top.
Step 4

Bake in preheated oven until the cheese is brown and bubbly, about 20 minutes.

Nutrition Facts

909 calories; protein 52.1g 104% DV; carbohydrates 77.6g 25% DV; fat 43g 66% DV; cholesterol 126.8mg 42% DV; sodium 2247.8mg 90% DV.

ITALIAN ONION CUCUMBER SALAD

Prep: 20 mins **Additional:** 1 hr - **Total:** 1 hr 20 mins - **Servings:** 4

INGREDIENTS

- 2 medium (blank)s cucumbers, cubed
- 1 red onion, diced
- 1 green bell pepper, diced
- 1 stalk celery, diced
- 1 tablespoon sea salt
- 1 teaspoon ground black pepper
- ½ (8 ounce) bottle zesty Italian-style salad dressing

DIRECTIONS

Step 1

Combine cucumbers, red onion, bell pepper, and celery in a large bowl; season with sea salt and black pepper. Pour dressing over cucumber mixture.

Step 2

Cover bowl with plastic wrap and refrigerate at least 1 hour.

Nutrition Facts

115.3 calories; protein 1.4g 3% DV; carbohydrates 11.1g 4% DV; fat 8.1g 12% DV; cholesterolmg; sodium 1789.5mg 72% DV.

AUNT RITA'S ITALIAN STEW

Prep: 30 mins - **Cook:** 30 mins - **Total:** 1 hr - **Servings:** 6

INGREDIENTS

- 1 pound mild Italian sausage links, cut into 1-inch pieces
- 1 cup chopped onion
- 1 tablespoon minced garlic
- 2 medium (blank)s yellow summer squash, thinly sliced
- 2 eaches zucchini, thinly sliced
- 2 carrot, (7-1/2")s carrots, thinly sliced
- 2 cups sliced fresh mushrooms

- 2 (14.5 ounce) cans Italian-style stewed tomatoes
- 2 tablespoons grated Parmesan cheese

DIRECTIONS

Step 1

Cook the sausage with onion and garlic in a large, deep skillet or pot over medium heat, until the meat is browned, 10 to 15 minutes, stirring frequently. Mix in the summer squash, zucchini, carrots, mushrooms, and stewed tomatoes, reduce heat to medium-low, and bring the mixture to a simmer. Cook, stirring occasionally, until the vegetables are tender, about 20 minutes. Sprinkle with Parmesan cheese, and serve.

Cook's Note

I use my food processor to slice all the vegetables.

Nutrition Facts

269.9 calories; protein 14.3g 29% DV; carbohydrates 20.7g 7% DV; fat 15.1g 23% DV; cholesterol 31.2mg 10% DV; sodium 967.8mg 39% DV.

QUICK BEAN AND TURKEY ITALIAN MEATBALLS

Prep: 20 mins - **Cook:** 10 mins - **Total:** 30 mins - **Servings:** 12

INGREDIENTS

- 1 (15 ounce) can butter beans, rinsed and drained
- 1 ¼ pounds extra-lean ground turkey breast
- 1 egg white, beaten
- 1 teaspoon onion powder
- ½ teaspoon garlic powder
- ½ teaspoon salt
- ¼ teaspoon black pepper
- ½ cup Italian bread crumbs
- 1 tablespoon olive oil

DIRECTIONS

Step 1

Mash butter beans in a large mixing bowl. Add ground turkey, egg white, onion powder, garlic powder, salt, and pepper; stir until evenly mixed. Fold bread crumbs into mixture evenly.

Step 2

Form the mixture into 1-inch meatballs.

Step 3

Heat oil in a skillet over medium heat.

Step 4

Cook meatballs in hot oil until browned on all sides, 5 to 7 minutes. Cover the skillet and continue cooking until meatballs are no longer pink in the center, about 5 minutes more. An instant-read thermometer inserted into the center should read at least 165 degrees F (74 degrees C).

Nutrition Facts

125.9 calories; protein 12.1g 24% DV; carbohydrates 8.1g 3% DV; fat 5g 8% DV; cholesterol 35mg 12% DV; sodium 340.4mg 14% DV.

ITALIAN NUTTHOUSE BROILED TOMATOES

Prep: 5 mins - **Cook:** 5 mins - **Total:** 10 mins - **Servings:** 4

INGREDIENTS

- 4 medium whole (2-3/5" dia) (blank)s tomatoes, cut into 1/4 inch slices
- ¼ cup olive oil
- 1 teaspoon kosher salt
- 1 teaspoon ground black pepper, or to taste
- 4 cloves garlic, minced
- 1 pinch monosodium glutamate (MSG)
- 3 tablespoons chopped fresh oregano
- ¾ cup freshly grated Parmesan cheese

DIRECTIONS

Step 1

Preheat your oven's broiler. Cover a broiler pan or baking sheet with aluminum foil, and coat with non-stick cooking spray.

Step 2

Arrange tomato slices in a single layer on the prepared baking sheet. Drizzle each slice lightly with olive oil, spreading oil evenly with finger if necessary. Season with salt, pepper, garlic, monosodium glutamate (if using), and oregano. Sprinkle Parmesan cheese over the top.

Step 3

Broil, 3 inches from the heat until cheese is browned and bubbly, 3 minutes.

Nutrition Facts

231.8 calories; protein 8.6g 17% DV; carbohydrates 7.4g 2% DV; fat 19.2g 30% DV; cholesterol 16.5mg 6% DV; sodium 805mg 32% DV.

NEW YORK ITALIAN STYLE CHEESECAKE

Prep: 20 mins - **Cook:** 1 hr **Additional:** 3 hrs - **Total:** 4 hrs 20 mins - **Servings:** 12

INGREDIENTS

- 1 pound cream cheese, softened
- 1 pound ricotta cheese
- 1 ½ cups white sugar
- 4 large eggs eggs
- ¼ cup butter, melted and cooled
- 3 tablespoons all-purpose flour
- 3 tablespoons cornstarch
- 2 ½ teaspoons vanilla extract
- 2 cups sour cream
- 2 tablespoons lemon juice

DIRECTIONS

Step 1

Preheat oven to 325 degrees F (165 degrees C). Move an oven rack to the middle of the oven.

Step 2

Beat the cream cheese, ricotta cheese, and sugar in a large mixing bowl with an electric mixer until well combined. Beat in the eggs, one at a time. Add the butter, flour, cornstarch, and vanilla extract; mix until well combined. Fold in the sour cream and lemon juice. Pour the mixture into an ungreased 10-inch springform pan.

Step 3

Bake in the preheated oven for 1 hour. Turn off the oven and leave the cheesecake in the oven for 2 more hours. Remove from oven and let cool completely. Run a thin spatula around the edge of the cheesecake before springing open the pan to remove. Serve at room temperature or cold; refrigerate leftovers.

Nutrition Facts

452.3 calories; protein 10.7g 21% DV; carbohydrates 32.6g 11% DV; fat 31.7g 49% DV; cholesterol 149.9mg 50% DV; sodium 215mg 9% DV.

ITALIAN CHEESECAKE

Prep: 30 mins - **Cook:** 50 mins **Additional:** 10 mins - **Total:** 1 hr 30 mins - **Servings:** 12

INGREDIENTS

- 1 ½ pounds ricotta cheese
- 2 cups confectioners' sugar
- 3 large eggs eggs
- 1 ½ teaspoons vanilla extract

- ½ teaspoon almond extract
- ½ teaspoon rum flavored extract
- 1 tablespoon grated lemon zest
- ¼ cup fresh lemon juice
- 1 tablespoon grated orange zest

DIRECTIONS

Step 1

Preheat oven to 400 degrees F (205 degrees C). Grease and flour one 9 inch round springform or regular pan.

Step 2

Combine the ricotta, confectioners' sugar and eggs. Blend well. Stir in vanilla, almond extract, rum extract, lemon juice, lemon zest and orange zest. Beat by hand until smooth and creamy. Pour batter into the prepared pan.

Step 3

Bake at 400 degrees F (205 degrees C) for 40 minutes, until golden. Place on a rack and cool.

Nutrition Facts

178.5 calories; protein 8.1g 16% DV; carbohydrates 23.6g 8% DV; fat 5.8g 9% DV; cholesterol 64.1mg 21% DV; sodium 88.8mg 4% DV.

ITALIAN STYLE BRUNCH CAKES

Prep: 10 mins - **Cook:** 20 mins - **Total:** 30 mins - **Servings:** 20

INGREDIENTS

- 2 cups biscuit baking mix
- ⅔ cup shredded Monterey Jack cheese
- 2 teaspoons Italian-style seasoning
- ½ cup diced red bell pepper
- ¼ cup sliced pepperoni sausage
- ¼ cup diced green onion
- ½ cup diced tomatoes
- ¼ cup diced green bell pepper
- ¼ cup pizza sauce
- ½ cup milk
- ½ cup nonfat sour cream
- 2 large eggs eggs, beaten

DIRECTIONS

Step 1

In a large bowl, combine baking mix, cheese, Italian-style seasoning, red bell pepper, pepperoni, green onion, tomatoes and green bell pepper.

Step 2

In a separate bowl, stir together pizza sauce, milk, sour cream and eggs. Stir egg mixture into flour/vegetable mixture until all flour is moistened.

Step 3

Heat a lightly oiled griddle or frying pan over medium high heat. Spoon the batter onto the griddle, using approximately 1 tablespoon for each pancake. Brown on both sides and serve hot.

Nutrition Facts

100.9 calories; protein 3.7g 7% DV; carbohydrates 10.2g 3% DV; fat 5g 8% DV; cholesterol 26.5mg 9% DV; sodium 286.6mg 12% DV.

CREAMY ITALIAN DRESSING II

Prep: 5 mins - **Total:** 5 mins - **Servings:** 8

INGREDIENTS

- ¾ cup mayonnaise
- 1 tablespoon red wine vinegar
- 1 tablespoon lemon juice
- 1 tablespoon vegetable oil
- 1 tablespoon water
- 1 teaspoon Worcestershire sauce
- ½ teaspoon dried oregano
- 1 teaspoon white sugar
- 1 clove garlic, chopped

DIRECTIONS

Step 1

In a small bowl, whisk together the mayonnaise, vinegar, lemon juice, oil, water, Worcestershire sauce, oregano, sugar and garlic until evenly combined. Chill before serving.

Nutrition Facts

167.6 calories; protein 0.2g 1% DV; carbohydrates 1.8g 1% DV; fat 18.1g 28% DV; cholesterol 7.8mg 3% DV; sodium 124.2mg 5% DV.

ITALIAN TOMATO CUCUMBER SALAD

Prep: 15 mins **Additional:** 30 mins - **Total:** 45 mins - **Servings:** 4

INGREDIENTS

- 4 eaches tomatoes on the vine, cored and chopped
- ½ red onion, thinly sliced
- ½ seedless English cucumber, chopped
- 3 tablespoons extra-virgin olive oil, or more if needed
- 1 tablespoon chopped fresh oregano
- 1 pinch salt and ground black pepper to taste

DIRECTIONS

Step 1

Mix tomatoes, red onion, cucumber, olive oil, oregano, salt, and black pepper together in a bowl; stir to coat. Let sit for 30 minutes to blend flavors.

Nutrition Facts

128 calories; protein 1.6g 3% DV; carbohydrates 8.1g 3% DV; fat 10.5g 16% DV; cholesterolmg; sodium 8.5mg.

ITALIAN-STYLE PORK TENDERLOIN

Prep: 20 mins - **Cook:** 30 mins **Additional:** 1 day - **Total:** 1 day

Servings: 4

INGREDIENTS

- 3 ½ pounds pork tenderloin
- 2 cloves garlic, minced
- 15 eaches oil-cured black olives, pitted
- 1 teaspoon prepared mustard
- salt and pepper to taste
- 1 red bell pepper, halved and deseeded
- 4 medium (blank)s fresh mushrooms
- 1 onion, thinly sliced
- 1 tablespoon browning sauce

DIRECTIONS

Step 1

Slice the pork tenderloin open the long way. Spread the mustard, minced garlic and chopped olives in the roast. Sprinkle with salt and pepper all-over, to taste. Tie the loin at 1-inch intervals to shape evenly into a roll. Refrigerate and marinate loin for 24 hours.

Step 2

To Grill: Prepare grill for high heat.

Step 3

Using a generous amount of heavy-duty foil, lay the sliced red pepper on the bottom. Put the marinated tenderloin on top. Paint the surface with browning sauce and place the onion slices and mushrooms on top. Seal the foil, making a little tent on top.

Step 4

Grill the pork for about 20 minutes or until it has reached an internal temperature of 145 degrees F (63 C). Remove from heat and allow the meat to rest for 10 minutes before slicing.

Step 5

To Bake: Preheat oven to 375 degrees F (190 degrees C).

Step 6

Lay the sliced red pepper on the bottom of a roasting pan. Put the marinated tenderloin on top. Paint the surface with browning sauce and place the onion slices and mushrooms on top. Cover and bake in the preheated oven for 30 minutes or until the internal temperature reaches 145 degrees F (63 degrees C). Let stand for 10 minutes before carving.

Nutrition Facts

532.4 calories; protein 83.3g 167% DV; carbohydrates 5.7g 2% DV; fat 17.1g 26% DV; cholesterol 258mg 86% DV; sodium 656.1mg 26% DV.

ITALIAN TURKEY ZOODLES

Prep: 15 mins - **Cook:** 38 mins **Additional:** 25 mins - **Total:** 1 hr 18 mins - **Servings:** 4

INGREDIENTS

- 3 medium (blank)s zucchini
- 1 tablespoon salt, or more as needed
- 1 pound ground turkey
- ½ teaspoon garlic salt
- ½ teaspoon garlic powder
- ½ teaspoon onion powder
- ¼ teaspoon cayenne pepper
- ¼ teaspoon red pepper flakes
- 1 teaspoon olive oil
- 1 teaspoon minced garlic
- 1 (14.5 ounce) can diced tomatoes
- 1 (3 ounce) can tomato paste
- 2 tablespoons balsamic vinegar
- 2 teaspoons dried parsley

- 1 teaspoon dried basil
- ½ teaspoon Italian seasoning
- ½ teaspoon salt
- ¼ teaspoon ground black pepper
- 1 cup small-curd cottage cheese
- 1 cup shredded mozzarella cheese

DIRECTIONS

Step 1
Make zucchini noodles using a spiralizer or julienne peeler. Place noodles in a colander and cover liberally with 1 tablespoon salt. Let sit until noodles release some moisture, about 20 minutes. Rinse noodles and pat dry.

Step 2
Place ground turkey, garlic salt, garlic powder, onion powder, cayenne pepper, and red pepper flakes in a large oven-safe skillet over medium heat. Cook and stir until turkey is browned and juices run clear, about 5 minutes. Drain grease.

Step 3
Push turkey to the sides of the skillet to make an empty space in the center. Add olive oil and minced garlic; cook until garlic is fragrant, about 1 minute.

Step 4
Preheat oven to 400 degrees F (200 degrees C).

Step 5
Stir diced tomatoes, tomato paste, balsamic vinegar, parsley, basil, Italian seasoning, 1/2 teaspoon salt, and black pepper into the skillet. Bring to a boil; cook until sauce thickens, about 15 minutes. Stir in noodles. Cover with cottage cheese. Sprinkle mozzarella cheese evenly on top.

Step 6
Bake in the preheated oven until cheese is melted, about 15 minutes. Turn on broiler and broil until cheese is golden brown, about 2 minutes. Remove from oven and let sit for 5 to 10 minutes before serving.

Cook's Notes:

Ricotta cheese can be used in the place of cottage cheese, and ground beef or ground chicken can replace the ground turkey if desired. Substitute 1 tablespoon chopped fresh basil for the dried if preferred.

A jar of spaghetti sauce can also be used in the place of the tomatoes, tomato paste, and spices to speed things up, but I don't feel that it's quite as good.

Editor's Note:

Nutrition data for this recipe includes the full amount of salt. The actual amount of salt consumed will vary.

Nutrition Facts

380.1 calories; protein 40.2g 80% DV; carbohydrates 17.1g 6% DV; fat 17.2g 27% DV; cholesterol 110.2mg 37% DV; sodium 3073.5mg 123% DV.

ITALIAN WEDDING COOKIES

Prep: 45 mins - **Cook**: 15 mins Additional: 20 mins - **Total**: 1 hr 20 mins - **Servings**: 40

INGREDIENTS

1 ½ cups unsalted butter

¾ cup confectioners' sugar

¾ teaspoon salt

1 ½ cups finely ground almonds

4 ½ teaspoons vanilla extract

3 cups sifted all-purpose flour

⅓ cup confectioners' sugar for rolling directions

Step 1

Preheat oven to 325 degrees F (165 degrees C).

Step 2

Cream butter or margarine in a bowl, gradually add confectioners' sugar and salt. Beat until light and fluffy. Add almonds and vanilla. Blend in flour gradually and mix well.

Step 3

Shape into balls (or crescents) using about 1 teaspoon for each Cookie. Place on ungreased Cookie sheets, and bake for 15-20 min. Do not brown. Cool slightly, then roll in the extra confectioners' sugar.

Nutrition Facts

140 calories; protein 2.2g 4% DV; carbohydrates 11.5g 4% DV; fat 9.7g 15% DV; cholesterol 18.3mg 6% DV; sodium 44.9mg 2% DV.

SLOW COOKER ITALIAN BEEF FOR SANDWICHES

Prep: 15 mins - **Cook**: 12 hrs - **Total**: 12 hrs 15 mins - **Servings**: 10

INGREDIENTS

- 3 cups water
- 1 teaspoon salt
- 1 teaspoon ground black pepper
- 1 teaspoon dried oregano
- 1 teaspoon dried basil
- 1 teaspoon onion salt
- 1 teaspoon dried parsley
- 1 teaspoon garlic powder

- 1 bay leaf
- 1 (.7 ounce) package dry Italian-style salad dressing mix
- 1 (5 pound) rump roast

DIRECTIONS

Step 1

Combine water with salt, ground black pepper, oregano, basil, onion salt, parsley, garlic powder, bay leaf, and salad dressing mix in a saucepan. Stir well, and bring to a boil.

Step 2

Place roast in slow Cooker, and pour salad dressing mixture over the meat.

Step 3

Cover, and Cook on Low for 10 to 12 hours, or on High for 4 to 5 hours. When done, remove bay leaf, and shred meat with a fork.

Nutrition Facts

318.2 calories; protein 39.4g 79% DV; carbohydrates 1.6g 1% DV; fat 15.8g 24% DV; cholesterol 100.4mg 34% DV; sodium 819.1mg 33% DV.

ITALIAN GRAVY

Prep: 45 mins - **Cook:** 5 hrs - **Total:** 5 hrs 45 mins - **Servings:** 12

INGREDIENTS

- 2 tablespoons extra virgin olive oil
- 1 large yellow onion, diced
- 1 clove garlic, minced
- 4 pounds pork shoulder roast
- ½ cup white wine
- 3 cups water
- 2 teaspoons dried oregano
- 2 teaspoons dried parsley
- 1 teaspoon dried thyme
- 1 teaspoon dried rosemary
- 3 tablespoons garlic powder
- 1 teaspoon salt
- 1 teaspoon black pepper
- 2 (28 ounce) cans tomato puree
- 6 cups water
- ¼ cup white sugar

DIRECTIONS

Step 1

Heat olive oil in a large stock pot over medium heat. Saute onions and garlic until lightly browned. Place pork shoulder in pot, and pour in 1/2 cup white wine and 3 cups water. In a small bowl, combine oregano, parsley, thyme, rosemary, garlic powder, salt and pepper. Sprinkle 1/4 of spice mixture over pork. Cover, and Cook for 30 minutes turning occasionally. Add water periodically if needed.

Step 2

Pour in tomato puree. Fill cans with water, and pour in (about 6 cups). Stir in remaining spice mixture and the sugar. When liquid starts to bubble, reduce heat to low, cover, and Cook for 4 to 5 hours. Stir occasionally, and adjust seasonings to taste.

Nutrition Facts

411.3 calories; protein 32.3g 65% DV; carbohydrates 19.4g 6% DV; fat 22.1g 34% DV; cholesterol 96.8mg 32% DV; sodium 794.4mg 32% DV.

ITALIAN SAUCE

Prep: 10 mins - **Cook:** 20 mins - **Total:** 30 mins - **Servings:** 16

INGREDIENTS

- 11 medium whole (2-3/5" dia) (blank)s tomatoes, coarsely chopped
- ½ cup red wine vinegar
- ½ cup white sugar
- 1 ½ teaspoons paprika
- ½ teaspoon salt
- ¼ teaspoon crushed garlic
- 1 tablespoon crushed red pepper
- 1 cinnamon stick
- 4 eaches whole cloves

DIRECTIONS

Step 1

Puree tomatoes in blender or food processor until smooth. Pour into a large saucepan with the red wine vinegar, sugar, paprika, salt, garlic, crushed red pepper, cinnamon stick and cloves. Simmer over medium-low heat, covered, until thickened and flavors have blended, 15 to 20 minutes. Remove cinnamon stick and cloves before serving.

Nutrition Facts

96.9 calories; protein 1.8g 4% DV; carbohydrates 18.6g 6% DV; fat 2.4g 4% DV; cholesterolmg; sodium 458.4mg 18% DV.

ITALIAN ENCHILADAS

Prep: 25 mins - **Cook:** 45 mins - **Total:** 1 hr 10 mins - **Servings:** 10

INGREDIENTS

- 2 pounds ground beef
- 1 large onion, chopped
- 2 (10.75 ounce) cans condensed cream of mushroom soup, undiluted
- 1 (1 pound) loaf processed cheese food, cut into thin slices
- 2 (26 ounce) cans marinara sauce
- 2 (6.5 ounce) cans tomato sauce
- ¾ cup water
- 20 (10 inch) flour tortillas

DIRECTIONS

Step 1

Preheat oven to 350 degrees F (175 degrees C).

Step 2

Place the ground beef and onion in a skillet over medium heat. Cook and stir until beef is evenly brown and onion is tender. Drain grease. Mix in soup, and continue Cooking until heated through.

Step 3

In a bowl, mix the marinara sauce, tomato sauce, and water. Spread 1/3 of the mixture across the bottom of a 9x13 inch baking pan. Fill each tortilla with about 2 tablespoons beef mixture and 2 slices cheese food (reserving enough cheese food slices for topping). Tightly roll each tortilla. Arrange tortillas in the pan in 2 layers, and cover completely with the remaining sauce mixture. Top with remaining cheese food.

Step 4

Cover with aluminum foil, and bake 45 minutes in the preheated oven, until bubbly.

Nutrition Facts

939 calories; protein 39.3g 79% DV; carbohydrates 102.9g 33% DV; fat 40.4g 62% DV; cholesterol 93.9mg 31% DV; sodium 2693.9mg 108% DV.

ITALIAN TACOS

Prep: 5 mins - **Cook:** 20 mins - **Total:** 25 mins - **Servings:** 16

INGREDIENTS

- ½ pound Italian sausage
- 1 pound ground beef
- 1 (16 ounce) jar tomato pasta sauce

- 1 teaspoon sugar
- 16 large (6-1/2" dia)s taco shells, heated
- 3 cups shredded mozzarella cheese
- 1 tablespoon dried Italian seasoning

DIRECTIONS

Step 1

Combine the ground beef and Italian sausage in a large heavy skillet. Cook over medium heat until evenly browned. Drain off excess grease, and season meat with Italian seasoning.

Step 2

Heat the pasta sauce in a saucepan over medium heat until heated through. When the sauce is warm, stir in the sugar.

Step 3

Fill taco shells with the meat mixture, spoon pasta sauce over, and top with mozzarella cheese.

Nutrition Facts

261.9 calories; protein 13.8g 28% DV; carbohydrates 18.5g 6% DV; fat 14.5g 22% DV; cholesterol 36.9mg 12% DV; sodium 461.7mg 19% DV.

ITALIAN PEAS

Prep: 5 mins - **Cook:** 10 mins - **Total:** 15 mins - **Servings:** 6

INGREDIENTS

- 2 tablespoons olive oil
- 1 onion, chopped
- 2 cloves garlic, minced
- 16 ounces frozen green peas
- 1 tablespoon chicken stock
- 1 pinch salt and ground black pepper to taste

DIRECTIONS

Step 1

Heat olive oil in a skillet over medium heat. Stir in onion; Cook until softened, about 5 minutes. Stir in garlic and Cook for 1 minute. Add frozen peas, and stir in stock. Season with salt and pepper. Cover, and Cook until the peas are tender, about 5 minutes.

Nutrition Facts

106.3 calories; protein 4.2g 8% DV; carbohydrates 12.3g 4% DV; fat 4.8g 7% DV; cholesterol 0.1mg; sodium 120.5mg 5% DV.

ITALIAN KALE

Prep: 5 mins - **Cook:** 15 mins - **Total:** 20 mins - **Servings:** 4

INGREDIENTS

- 1 bunch kale, stems removed and leaves coarsely chopped
- 1 clove garlic, minced
- 1 tablespoon olive oil
- 2 tablespoons balsamic vinegar
- 1 dash Salt and ground black pepper to taste

DIRECTIONS

Step 1

Cook the kale in a large, covered saucepan over medium-high heat until the leaves wilt. Once the volume of the kale is reduced by half, uncover and stir in the garlic, olive oil and vinegar. Cook while stirring for 2 more minutes. Add salt and pepper to taste.

Nutrition Facts

92.4 calories; protein 3.8g 8% DV; carbohydrates 12.6g 4% DV; fat 4.2g 6% DV; cholesterolmg; sodium 147.1mg 6% DV.

ITALIAN WEDDING SOUP

Prep: 20 mins - **Cook:** 30 mins - **Total:** 50 mins - **Servings:** 4

INGREDIENTS

- ½ pound extra-lean ground beef
- 1 egg, lightly beaten
- 2 tablespoons dry bread crumbs
- 1 tablespoon grated Parmesan cheese
- ½ teaspoon dried basil
- ½ teaspoon onion powder
- 5 ¾ cups chicken broth
- 2 cups thinly sliced escarole
- 1 cup unCooked orzo pasta
- ⅓ cup finely chopped carrot

DIRECTIONS

Step 1

In medium bowl, combine meat, egg, bread crumbs, cheese, basil and onion powder; shape into 3/4 inch balls.

Step 2

In large saucepan, heat broth to boiling; stir in escarole, orzo pasta, chopped carrot and meatballs. Return to boil, then reduce heat to medium. Cook at slow boil for 10 minutes, or until pasta is al dente. Stir frequently to prevent sticking.

Nutrition Facts

416.3 calories; protein 27.3g 55% DV; carbohydrates 43.3g 14% DV; fat 14.2g 22% DV; cholesterol 86.8mg 29% DV; sodium 1211mg 48% DV.

ITALIAN RIB EYE

Prep: 15 mins - **Cook:** 15 mins Additional: 1 hr - **Total:** 1 hr 30 mins - **Servings:** 3

INGREDIENTS

- 10 cloves garlic, roughly chopped
- 1 tablespoon chopped fresh oregano
- 1 tablespoon chopped fresh basil
- 1 tablespoon chopped fresh parsley
- 1 teaspoon chopped fresh rosemary
- 1 tablespoon kosher salt
- ½ cup olive oil
- 2 tablespoons balsamic vinegar
- 1 teaspoon white pepper
- 3 (10 ounce) boneless beef ribeye steaks, cut 1 inch thick

DIRECTIONS

Step 1

Place the garlic, oregano, basil, parsley, rosemary, and salt into a mortar or small bowl, and mash into a coarse paste. Stir in the olive oil, balsamic vinegar, and white pepper until evenly blended. Scrape half of the mixture into a separate small bowl; set aside. Spread the remaining half of the herb mixture evenly over the steaks. Set aside to marinate for 1 hour.

Step 2

Preheat an outdoor grill for medium-high heat, and lightly oil the grate.

Step 3

Cook the steaks on the preheated grill for 7 minutes, then turn over, and coat with the reserved herb mixture. Continue Cooking 7 minutes more for medium-well, or until your desired degree of doneness has been reached.

Nutrition Facts

1077.8 calories; protein 50.7g 101% DV; carbohydrates 5.7g 2% DV; fat 93.9g 145% DV; cholesterol 187.6mg 63% DV; sodium 2082.7mg 83% DV.

ITALIAN COOKIES II

Prep: 30 mins - **Cook:** 10 mins Additional: 5 mins - **Total:** 45 mins - **Servings:** 36

INGREDIENTS

- ½ cup butter, softened
- 1 cup white sugar
- 2 large eggs eggs
- 1 teaspoon vanilla extract
- 8 ounces ricotta cheese
- 2 cups all-purpose flour
- ½ teaspoon baking soda
- ¼ teaspoon salt
- 2 tablespoons butter, softened
- 2 cups confectioners' sugar
- ¼ teaspoon vanilla extract
- 1 ½ tablespoons milk

DIRECTIONS

Step 1

Preheat oven to 350 degrees F (175 degrees C). Grease Cookie sheets.

Step 2

In a medium bowl, cream together 1/2 cup butter and white sugar until smooth. Beat in the eggs one at a time, then stir in the vanilla and ricotta cheese. Combine the flour, baking soda and salt; gradually stir into the cheese mixture. Drop by rounded teaspoonfuls 2 inches apart onto the prepared Cookie sheets.

Step 3

Bake for 8 to 10 minutes in the preheated oven, or until edges are golden. Allow Cookies to cool on baking sheet for 5 minutes before removing to a wire rack to cool completely.

Step 4

In a medium bowl, cream together the remaining butter and confectioners' sugar. Beat in vanilla and milk gradually until a spreadable consistency is reached. Frost cooled Cookies.

Nutrition Facts

114.4 calories; protein 1.8g 4% DV; carbohydrates 17.9g 6% DV; fat 4.1g 6% DV; cholesterol 20.8mg 7% DV; sodium 68.6mg 3% DV.

JOHNSONVILLE ITALIAN MEATBALLS

Prep: 25 mins - **Cook:** 20 mins - **Total:** 45 mins - **Servings:** 6

INGREDIENTS

- 1 egg, lightly beaten
- ⅓ cup dry bread crumbs
- ¼ cup KRAFT 100% Grated Parmesan Cheese
- ¼ cup milk
- ¼ cup finely chopped onion
- 1 (19 ounce) package Johnsonville Ground Mild Italian Sausage or Links, casings removed*

DIRECTIONS

Step 1

Preheat oven to 350 degrees F.

Step 2

In a large bowl, combine the egg, bread crumbs, Parmesan cheese, milk and onion.

Step 3

Remove sausage from casings. Add sausage to the bread crumb mixture and mix well. Shape into 20 meatballs. Arrange meatballs on a shallow baking pan.

Step 4

Bake for 20 minutes or until meatballs are Cooked through (160 degrees F). Serve with your favorite sauce and spaghetti.

Nutrition Facts

366.4 calories; protein 18.7g 37% DV; carbohydrates 6.6g 2% DV; fat 29g 45% DV; cholesterol 104.6mg 35% DV; sodium 975.8mg 39% DV.

OLD ITALIAN MEAT SAUCE

Prep: 30 mins - **Cook:** 4 hrs - **Total:** 4 hrs 30 mins - **Servings:** 20

INGREDIENTS

- 2 pounds lean ground beef
- 1 pound ground pork
- 2 tablespoons olive oil
- 2 medium (2-1/2" dia)s onions, chopped
- 1 clove garlic, crushed
- 3 cups red wine
- 2 pounds fresh mushrooms, sliced
- ¼ teaspoon dried rosemary
- 4 tablespoons chopped fresh oregano
- ¼ teaspoon chopped fresh thyme

- 3 (29 ounce) cans tomato sauce
- 1 (6 ounce) can tomato paste
- 2 tablespoons grated Parmesan cheese

DIRECTIONS

Step 1

In a large skillet, brown beef and pork over medium heat until no longer pink; set aside.

Step 2

In a large skillet, warm olive oil over medium heat and saute onions and garlic until tender; add about 1/2 cup of wine; mix well.

Step 3

Add mushrooms, rosemary, oregano and thyme to skillet and add another 1/2 cup wine; saute until tender.

Step 4

Add browned meat, tomato sauce and tomato paste to mixture; simmer for 1 hour and add the remaining 2 cups of wine.

Step 5

Nutrition Facts

295.9 calories; protein 15.2g 30% DV; carbohydrates 15.9g 5% DV; fat 16.8g 26% DV; cholesterol 50.8mg 17% DV; sodium 788.1mg 32% DV.

SOUTHERN ITALIAN THANKSGIVING STUFFING

Prep: 45 mins - **Cook:** 1 hr 15 mins - **Total:** 2 hrs - **Servings:** 12

INGREDIENTS

- 1 ½ pounds bulk Italian sausage
- 2 tablespoons olive oil
- 6 ounces pancetta bacon, diced
- 2 medium (2-1/2" dia)s onions, chopped
- 7 large stalks celery, chopped
- 4 cloves garlic, minced
- 6 cups day-old French bread, cut into 1/2 inch cubes
- 3 cups crumbled cornbread
- 1 ½ tablespoons rubbed dried sage
- 1 ½ tablespoons poultry seasoning
- 1 teaspoon salt
- 1 cup toasted pine nuts

- 4 cups chicken broth
- 2 cups shredded mozzarella cheese
- ½ cup butter
- 2 tablespoons chopped fresh sage
- 1 ounce shaved Parmesan cheese

DIRECTIONS

Step 1

Preheat an oven to 375 degrees F (190 degrees C). Grease a deep 9x13 inch baking dish or roasting pan.

Step 2

Heat a large skillet over medium-high heat and stir in the sausage. Cook and stir until the sausage is crumbly, evenly browned, and no longer pink. Drain and discard any excess grease. Place the browned sausage into a large mixing bowl.

Step 3

Meanwhile, heat the olive oil and pancetta in a large skillet over medium heat. Once the pancetta begins to brown, stir in the onions and celery, and Cook until the onion softens and turns translucent, about 8 minutes. Stir in the garlic, and Cook another 3 minutes until the aroma of the garlic mellows.

Step 4

Scrape the onion mixture into the bowl with the crumbled sausage. Add the French bread, cornbread, dried sage, poultry seasoning, salt, and pine nuts; stir well. Pour in the chicken broth and mozzarella cheese; stir until the chicken stock has been absorbed by the bread and the stuffing is evenly mixed. Pack the stuffing into the prepared baking dish, and dot the butter overtop. Cover with aluminum foil.

Step 5

Bake in the preheated oven for 45 minutes, then remove the foil, and continue baking until the top has turned golden brown, about 15 minutes more. Sprinkle with the fresh sage and shaved Parmesan cheese to serve.

Nutrition Facts

594.3 calories; protein 25.9g 52% DV; carbohydrates 45.3g 15% DV; fat 34.8g 54% DV; cholesterol 70.5mg 24% DV; sodium 1794.8mg 72% DV.

QUICK ITALIAN SKILLET DINNER

Prep: 10 m - **Cook:** 20 m **Ready In:** 30 m

INGREDIENTS

- 1 pound Italian sausage
- 1/2 cup chopped green bell pepper
- 1 medium onion, chopped
- 1 (14.5 ounce) can RED GOLD Diced Tomatoes

- 2 cups RED GOLD Vegetable Juice from Concentrate
- 1 1/2 cups instant rice
- 1 cup shredded mozzarella cheese
- Add all ingredients to list

DIRECTIONS

Step 1

In large skillet Cook sausage until no longer pink, 4 to 6 minutes. Drain off excess fat. Add green bell pepper and onion; Cook until crisp.

Step 2

Add diced tomatoes and vegetable juice; Cook and stir until mixture boils. Remove from heat and stir in rice.

Step 3

Cover and let stand 6 to 8 minutes or until liquid is absorbed.

Step 4

Sprinkle with cheese; cover and let stand until cheese is melted.

Cooking Hint:

Yields differ between regular rice and instant rice. One cup of unCooked regular rice equals 3 cups Cooked and 1 cup of instant rice equals 2 cups Cooked.

Nutrition Facts

Per Serving: 358 calories; 17.5 g fat; 30.7 g carbohydrates; 17.9 g protein; 42 mg cholesterol; 1012 mg sodium.

ITALIAN STUFFED CHICKEN BREAST

Prep: 20 mins - **Cook:** 50 mins - **Total:** 1 hr 10 mins - **Servings:** 4

INGREDIENTS

- 1 ½ cups shredded Italian cheese blend
- 1 clove garlic, finely chopped
- 1 teaspoon dried basil
- 1 teaspoon dried oregano
- ½ cup grated Parmesan cheese
- ½ cup Italian-seasoned bread crumbs
- 4 eaches boneless, skinless chicken breasts
- 1 egg, well beaten
- 1 cup spaghetti sauce
- ¼ cup shredded Italian cheese blend, or to taste

DIRECTIONS

Step 1

Preheat oven to 350 degrees F (175 degrees C).

Step 2

Combine 1 1/2 cup Italian cheese blend, garlic, basil, and oregano in a bowl. Combine Parmesan cheese and bread crumbs in a separate bowl.

Step 3

Cut one side of each chicken breast through the middle horizontally to within one-half inch of the other side. Open the two sides and spread them out like an open book. Lightly pound chicken to flatten. Fill each chicken breast with Italian cheese blend mixture and close like a book over the filling. Coat the outside of each chicken breast with egg; press bread crumb mixture over egg layer to coat each chicken breast. Arrange chicken breasts in a 9x13-inch baking dish.

Step 4

Bake in the preheated oven until chicken is no longer pink in the center and the juices run clear, about 45 minutes. An instant-read thermometer inserted into the center should read at least 165 degrees F (74 degrees C). Pour spaghetti sauce over Cooked chicken; top with 1/4 cup Italian cheese blend. Bake until sauce is bubbling and cheese is melted, about 5 more minutes.

Nutrition Facts

470.1 calories; protein 43.5g 87% DV; carbohydrates 21.5g 7% DV; fat 22.7g 35% DV; cholesterol 154.5mg 52% DV; sodium 1007.7mg 40% DV.

ITALIAN PASTA SALAD I

Prep: 15 mins - **Cook:** 15 mins - **Total:** 30 mins - **Servings:** 12

INGREDIENTS

- 1 (16 ounce) package rotini pasta
- 1 cup Italian-style salad dressing
- 1 cup creamy Caesar salad dressing
- 1 cup grated Parmesan cheese
- 1 red bell pepper, diced
- 1 green bell pepper, chopped
- 1 red onion, diced

DIRECTIONS

Step 1

In a large pot of salted boiling water, Cook pasta until al dente, rinse under cold water and drain.

Step 2

In a large bowl, combine the pasta, Italian salad dressing, Caesar dressing, Parmesan cheese, red bell pepper, green bell pepper, and red onion. Mix well and serve chilled or at room temperature.

Nutrition Facts

290.6 calories; protein 8.5g 17% DV; carbohydrates 32.6g 11% DV; fat 14.6g 23% DV; cholesterol 5.9mg 2% DV; sodium 728.2mg 29% DV.

SPECIAL ITALIAN EASTER PIZZA

Prep: 40 mins - **Cook:** 50 mins **Additional:** 25 mins - **Total:** 1 hr 55 mins - **Servings:** 10

INGREDIENTS

- ½ pound bulk Italian sausage
- 2 teaspoons olive oil
- 1 (1 pound) loaf frozen bread dough, thawed
- ½ pound sliced mozzarella cheese
- ½ pound sliced Cooked ham
- ½ pound sliced provolone cheese
- ½ pound sliced salami
- ½ pound sliced pepperoni
- 1 (16 ounce) container ricotta cheese
- ½ cup grated Parmesan cheese
- 8 large eggs eggs, beaten
- 1 egg
- 1 teaspoon water

DIRECTIONS

Step 1

Cook and stir Italian sausage in a skillet over medium heat, breaking the sausage into crumbles as it Cooks, until well browned, 5 to 8 minutes. Drain excess grease; set sausage aside.

Step 2

Preheat oven to 350 degrees F (175 degrees C).

Step 3

Oil the bottom and sides of a 10-inch springform pan with olive oil.

Step 4

Cut 1/3 of the dough off the loaf and set aside under a cloth. Form the remaining 2/3 dough into a ball and roll into a 14-inch circle on a floured work surface.

Step 5

Line the springform pan with rolled dough, allowing dough to hang over the edge by 2 inches all around.

Step 6

Layer half the Cooked Italian sausage, half the mozzarella cheese, half the ham, half the provolone cheese, half the salami, and half the pepperoni into the pie crust.

Step 7

Spoon and spread half the ricotta cheese over the layers of meat and cheeses.

Step 8

Sprinkle half the Parmesan cheese over the ricotta.

Step 9

Pour half the 8 beaten eggs over the layers; continue layering the remaining meats, sliced cheeses, ricotta cheese, and then Parmesan cheese.

Step 10

Pour remaining beaten eggs over the last layer of Parmesan cheese.

Step 11

Roll out remaining piece of bread dough to a circle about 12 inches in diameter; lay the piece over the pie to form the top crust. Roll and pinch the bottom crust overhang over the top crust to seal in the filling.

Step 12

Beat 1 egg with water in a small bowl; brush the top of the pie with egg wash.

Step 13

Bake pie in the preheated oven until the crust is golden brown and the filling is set, 50 to 60 minutes. A toothpick inserted into the middle of the crust should come out without raw egg.

Step 14

Allow pie to cool in the pan for at least 25 minutes before releasing the spring and removing pie from the pan. Transfer to a serving platter and cut into wedges for serving.

Cook's Note:

In many traditional Italian homes this recipe calls for the addition of hard-boiled eggs. They can be added to this recipe - simply slice 4 hard boiled eggs and layer with the meats and cheeses; bake like normal.

Nutrition Facts

707.3 calories; protein 45.4g 91% DV; carbohydrates 28.1g 9% DV; fat 44.6g 69% DV; cholesterol 283.5mg 95% DV; sodium 2090.3mg 84% DV.

QUICK ITALIAN VEGETABLE SOUP

Prep: 15 mins - **Cook:** 30 mins - **Total:** 45 mins - **Servings:** 6

INGREDIENTS

- 1 tablespoon olive oil
- 1 medium onion, chopped
- 2 thin strips carrots, sliced
- 2 stalks celery, sliced
- 1 (16 ounce) can diced plum tomatoes

- 2 teaspoons Italian seasoning
- 2 cubes beef bouillon
- 6 cups water
- 2 medium (blank)s zucchinis, quartered and sliced
- 2 cups sliced cabbage
- 1 teaspoon garlic salt
- 1 teaspoon salt and ground black pepper to taste
- ½ cup freshly grated Parmesan cheese

DIRECTIONS

Step 1

Heat oil in a large stock pot over medium-high heat. Saute onion, carrot, and celery until onion is translucent and vegetables are tender, 5 to 7 minutes. Stir in tomatoes and Italian seasoning, and Cook 5 minutes more, stirring frequently.

Step 2

Dissolve bouillon cubes in water, and stir into vegetables. Adjust heat to a medium simmer, and Cook approximately 10 minutes. Add zucchini and cabbage, sprinkle with garlic salt, and Cook until tender, 5 minutes more. Adjust seasoning with salt and pepper, and serve.

Nutrition Facts

93 calories; protein 4.9g 10% DV; carbohydrates 10g 3% DV; fat 4.5g 7% DV; cholesterol 5.9mg 2% DV; sodium 1210.2mg 48% DV.

ITALIAN HALIBUT CHOWDER

Prep: 20 mins - **Cook:** 1 hr 10 mins - **Total:** 1 hr 30 mins - **Servings:** 8

INGREDIENTS

- 2 ½ pounds halibut steaks, cubed
- 1 red bell pepper, chopped
- 1 onion, chopped
- 3 stalks celery, chopped
- 3 cloves garlic, minced
- ¼ cup olive oil
- 1 cup tomato juice
- ½ cup apple juice
- 2 (16 ounce) cans whole peeled tomatoes, mashed
- 2 tablespoons chopped fresh parsley
- ½ teaspoon salt

- ½ teaspoon dried basil
- ⅛ teaspoon dried thyme
- ⅛ teaspoon ground black pepper

DIRECTIONS

Step 1

Saute the peppers, celery, onion, and garlic in oil until tender. Add the tomato juice or water, apple juice, mashed tomatoes, and herbs. Simmer for 30 minutes.

Step 2

Add halibut pieces to the soup. Cook until halibut is done, about 30 minutes. Salt and pepper to taste.

Nutrition Facts

262.1 calories; protein 31.2g 62% DV; carbohydrates 10.7g 4% DV; fat 10.3g 16% DV; cholesterol 45.4mg 15% DV; sodium 399.7mg 16% DV.

BOWTIES AND ITALIAN SAUSAGE

Prep: 15 mins - **Cook:** 20 mins - **Total:** 35 mins - **Servings:** 6

INGREDIENTS

- 1 (12 ounce) package bow-tie pasta
- 1 tablespoon olive oil
- 18 ounces sweet Italian sausage, cut into bite-sized pieces
- 2 eaches red bell pepper, chopped
- 1 onion, chopped
- 1 (14 ounce) can diced tomatoes
- 1 (14 ounce) can beef broth
- ½ teaspoon Italian seasoning

DIRECTIONS

Step 1

Bring a large pot of lightly salted water to a boil. Cook the bow-tie pasta at a boil, stirring occasionally, until about halfway Cooked, 5 to 6 minutes; drain.

Step 2

Heat olive oil in a skillet over medium heat; Cook and stir sausage in the hot oil until browned and Cooked through, 5 to 10 minutes. Add red bell pepper and onion; Cook and stir until onion is softened, 5 to 10 minutes.

Step 3

Stir tomatoes, beef broth, and Italian seasoning through the sausage mixture; bring to a simmer. Add bow-tie pasta to the sausage-broth mixture; simmer until pasta is Cooked yet firm to the bite, 5 to 6 more minutes.

Nutrition Facts

463.2 calories; protein 20.6g 41% DV; carbohydrates 51.9g 17% DV; fat 19.7g 30% DV; cholesterol 33mg 11% DV; sodium 1014.4mg 41% DV.

ITALIAN STEWED TOMATOES

Prep: 30 mins - **Cook:** 10 mins - **Total:** 40 mins - **Servings:** 9

INGREDIENTS

- 24 large tomatoes - peeled, seeded and chopped
- 1 cup chopped celery
- ½ cup chopped onion
- ¼ cup chopped green bell pepper
- 2 teaspoons dried basil
- 1 tablespoon white sugar

DIRECTIONS

Step 1

In a large saucepan over medium heat, combine tomatoes, celery, onion, bell pepper, basil and sugar. Cover and Cook for 10 minutes, stirring occasionally to prevent sticking.

Nutrition Facts

100.5 calories; protein 4.6g 9% DV; carbohydrates 22.2g 7% DV; fat 1g 2% DV; cholesterolmg; sodium 34.4mg 1% DV.

ITALIAN NACHOS RESTAURANT-STYLE

Prep: 15 mins - **Cook:** 10 mins - **Total:** 25 mins - **Servings:** 8

INGREDIENTS

- 1 pound bulk Italian sausage
- 1 (7-1/2 ounce) bag tortilla chips
- 1 (2 ounce) package sliced pepperoni
- ½ pound shredded mozzarella cheese
- ½ cup banana peppers, drained
- 1 ¼ cups pizza sauce

DIRECTIONS

Step 1

Preheat your oven's broiler.

Step 2

Crumble the sausage into a large skillet over medium heat. Cook and stir until no longer pink; drain.

Step 3

Arrange the tortilla chips on a baking sheet. Top with sausage, pepperoni, mozzarella cheese, and banana peppers. Place nachos under the preheated broiler until the cheese is melted, 5 to 8 minutes. Serve with pizza sauce for dipping.

Nutrition Facts

453.4 calories; protein 19.3g 39% DV; carbohydrates 22.5g 7% DV; fat 31.7g 49% DV; cholesterol 68.7mg 23% DV; sodium 1132.7mg 45% DV.

ITALIAN SAUSAGE - TUSCAN STYLE

Prep: 30 mins **Additional:** 1 hr 30 mins **- Total:** 2 hrs **- Servings:** 20

INGREDIENTS

- 4 pounds coarse ground pork shoulder
- 1 pound coarse ground pork back fat
- 2 tablespoons salt
- 2 tablespoons white sugar
- 1 ½ teaspoons coarsely ground black pepper
- 1 teaspoon garlic powder
- ¾ teaspoon ground mace
- ½ teaspoon ground coriander
- ¼ teaspoon ground cayenne pepper
- ½ cup ice water
- 80 eaches inches sausage casing, 1 1/2 inches wide

DIRECTIONS

Step 1

Using a spice grinder or food processor, pulverize the salt, black pepper and sugar. In a large bowl, mix together the pork shoulder, back fat, garlic powder, mace, coriander, cayenne and ice water. Mix in the salt, pepper and sugar. Use latex gloves when mixing to avoid contamination of the meat, and keep the mixture cold.

Step 2

Stuff the sausage mixture into the casings and twist off in 3 inch lengths. If you do not have a stuffer, the sausage can be formed into patties or rolled into logs. Refrigerate and use up in one week or freeze for up to 6 weeks.

Nutrition Facts

371.8 calories; protein 18.4g 37% DV; carbohydrates 1.5g 1% DV; fat 31.9g 49% DV; cholesterol 71mg 24% DV; sodium 746.8mg 30% DV.

ITALIAN-STYLE STRAWBERRY SHORTCAKE

Prep: 15 mins - **Total:** 15 mins - **Servings:** 12

INGREDIENTS

- 1 quart ripe strawberries, sliced
- ⅓ cup white sugar, or to taste
- 1 (8 ounce) container mascarpone cheese
- 1 (8 ounce) container frozen whipped topping (such as Cool Whip), thawed
- 1 (10 inch) prepared angel food cake, torn into bite-size pieces

DIRECTIONS

Step 1

Set aside a few pretty strawberry slices for garnish; sprinkle remaining strawberries with sugar in a bowl and let stand for 10 minutes for juice to form.

Step 2

Mix mascarpone cheese and whipped topping together in a separate bowl. Place torn pieces of angel food cake into a trifle dish; spread strawberries and their juice on cake pieces and top with mascarpone mixture. Decorate with retained strawberry slices. Refrigerate until serving time.

Nutrition Facts

249.5 calories; protein 3.6g 7% DV; carbohydrates 30g 10% DV; fat 13.8g 21% DV; cholesterol 23.3mg 8% DV; sodium 224.9mg 9% DV.

ITALIAN SAUSAGE AND BEAN SOUP

Prep: 20 mins - **Cook:** 25 mins - **Total:** 45 mins - **Servings:** 4

INGREDIENTS

- 1 pound Italian turkey sausage, casings removed
- 2 medium (blank)s carrots, thinly sliced
- 1 large onion, chopped
- 1 cup thinly sliced mushrooms
- ⅓ cup chopped fresh parsley, divided
- 1 clove garlic, minced
- 3 cups water
- 1 (15 ounce) can garbanzo beans (chickpeas)
- 2 cubes beef bouillon
- ½ teaspoon dried sage

- 1 pinch salt and ground black pepper to taste

DIRECTIONS

Step 1

Heat a pot over medium heat. Cook and stir turkey sausage in the hot pot until browned and crumbly, 5 to 7 minutes.

Step 2

Stir carrots, onion, mushrooms, 1/4 cup parsley, and garlic into sausage. Cook and stir until onion is soft, 7 to 10 minutes.

Step 3

Pour water, garbanzo beans with liquid, beef bouillon cubes, and sage into sausage mixture. Bring to a boil, cover the pot, reduce heat to low, and simmer until carrots are tender, about 10 minutes. Skim and discard any accumulated fat. Season with salt and pepper; garnish with remaining 4 teaspoons parsley.

Nutrition Facts

306.1 calories; protein 26.3g 53% DV; carbohydrates 23.7g 8% DV; fat 12.4g 19% DV; cholesterol 85.7mg 29% DV; sodium 1612.8mg 65% DV.

GRANNY'S ITALIAN ZUCCHINI PIE

Prep: 15 mins **- Cook:** 30 mins **- Total:** 45 mins **- Servings:** 8

INGREDIENTS

- ¼ cup butter
- 4 cups thinly sliced zucchini
- 1 cup coarsely chopped onion
- ½ teaspoon salt
- ½ teaspoon ground black pepper
- ½ teaspoon garlic powder
- ½ teaspoon dried basil
- ½ teaspoon dried oregano
- 2 large eggs eggs, well beaten
- 1 (8 ounce) package shredded mozzarella cheese
- 1 (8 ounce) tube refrigerated crescent rolls
- 2 tablespoons yellow mustard

DIRECTIONS

Step 1

Preheat the oven to 375 degrees F (190 degrees C).

Step 2

Heat butter in a skillet over medium heat; Cook and stir zucchini and onion until tender, about 10 minutes.

Add salt, pepper, garlic powder, basil, and oregano; stir to coat.

Step 3

Whisk eggs and mozzarella cheese together in a bowl. Stir zucchini mixture into egg mixture.

Step 4

Separate crescent dough into two rectangles and place into a 8x12-inch baking dish; press into bottom and slightly up sides of dish to form a crust. Spread mustard onto crust. Pour zucchini-egg mixture into crust.

Step 5

Bake in the preheated oven until set in the middle and lightly browned, 18 to 20 minutes. Cool before cutting into squares or wedges.

Nutrition Facts

270.9 calories; protein 11.6g 23% DV; carbohydrates 16.2g 5% DV; fat 17.7g 27% DV; cholesterol 79.7mg 27% DV; sodium 647.4mg 26% DV.

ITALIAN SPAGHETTI SQUASH

Prep: 15 mins - **Cook:** 1 hr 25 mins - **Total:** 1 hr 40 mins - **Servings:** 4

INGREDIENTS

- ½ cup water
- 1 spaghetti squash, halved and seeded
- 2 tablespoons butter
- 1 tablespoon olive oil
- 1 onion, diced
- 1 clove garlic, minced
- 1 (14.5 ounce) can diced tomatoes with onion, celery, and green pepper
- 2 teaspoons dried basil
- 1 teaspoon salt
- 1 teaspoon ground black pepper
- ¼ cup shredded Parmesan cheese, plus more for topping

DIRECTIONS

Step 1

Preheat oven to 350 degrees F (175 degrees C).

Step 2

Pour water in baking dish and place halved squash cut-sides down in the dish.

Step 3

Bake squash in preheated oven until a fork pierces the skin very easily, about 45 minutes. Let squash cook while preparing remainder of recipe.

Step 4

Melt butter with olive oil in a large skillet over medium-high heat. Saute onion in hot butter until softened, about 5 minutes. Add garlic and continue to saute until fragrant, about 1 minute more. Pour diced tomatoes over the onion mixture; season with basil. Place a cover on the skillet, reduce heat to medium-low, and cook at a simmer until the tomatoes are soft, about 30 minutes; season with salt and pepper.

Step 5

Once squash is cool enough to handle, use a fork to strip flesh from the skin in strands. Stir squash and Parmesan cheese into tomato mixture. Replace cover on skillet and cook until squash is heated through, 5 to 10 minutes more. Sprinkle additional Parmesan cheese over the dish to serve.

Nutrition Facts

204.5 calories; protein 5.2g 11% DV; carbohydrates 22.4g 7% DV; fat 12.5g 19% DV; cholesterol 19.7mg 7% DV; sodium 1229.8mg 49% DV.

SIMPLE ITALIAN OMELET

Prep: 10 mins - **Cook:** 5 mins - **Total:** 15 mins - **Servings:** 1

INGREDIENTS

- 2 tablespoons olive oil
- 3 large eggs eggs, beaten
- 1 tablespoon crumbled goat cheese, or to taste
- 2 teaspoons chopped chives, divided, or to taste
- 1 pinch sea salt and ground black pepper to taste

DIRECTIONS

Step 1

Heat olive oil in a large skillet over medium heat, swirling oil to coat the skillet. Pour eggs into hot skillet; eggs will bubble and firm immediately.

Step 2

Lift cooked edges of the omelet with a rubber spatula and tilt the skillet so that the uncooked egg runs underneath the lifted edge. Continue cooking, lifting edges and tilting the skillet, until omelet is almost completely set, 1 to 2 minutes total cooking time; remove from heat. Spread out any runny egg evenly on the top of the omelet with a rubber spatula.

Step 3

Sprinkle goat cheese, 1 1/2 teaspoons chives, sea salt, and black pepper over omelet. Gently lift one edge and fold 1/3 of the omelet into the center over the cheese and chives. Fold the opposite 1/3 of the omelet into the center. Slide omelet to the edge of the skillet and flip, folded side down, onto a plate. Top with remaining chives.

Nutrition Facts

479.5 calories; protein 20.5g 41% DV; carbohydrates 1.4g 1% DV; fat 44g 68% DV; cholesterol 563.6mg

188% DV; sodium 567mg 23% DV.

ITALIAN BUTTERBALL COOKIES

Prep: 15 mins - **Cook:** 10 mins **Additional:** 30 mins - **Total:** 55 mins - **Servings:** 48

INGREDIENTS

- 1 stick butter
- ¾ cup confectioners' sugar
- 1 egg
- 1 teaspoon vanilla extract
- 1 teaspoon almond extract
- 1 ½ cups all-purpose flour
- 2 teaspoons baking powder
- 1 pinch salt
- ¼ cup confectioners' sugar

DIRECTIONS

Step 1

Preheat an oven to 350 degrees F (175 degrees C). Grease a baking sheet.

Step 2

Beat together the butter and 3/4 cup confectioners' sugar with an electric mixer in a large bowl until smooth. Add the egg, vanilla extract, and almond extract. Stir together the flour, baking powder, and salt in a bowl and mix into the butter mixture until just incorporated. Shape the dough into 1-inch balls and arrange on the prepared baking sheet spaced about 2 inches apart.

Step 3

Bake in the preheated oven until firm, about 10 minutes. Cool on the sheet for 10 minutes before removing to cool completely on a wire rack.

Step 4

Spread the 1/4 cup confectioners sugar on a plate; roll the cooled cookies in the confectioners' sugar to coat.

Nutrition Facts

43.3 calories; protein 0.6g 1% DV; carbohydrates 5.6g 2% DV; fat 2.1g 3% DV; cholesterol 9mg 3% DV; sodium 35.5mg 1% DV.

ITALIAN FIG COOKIES II

Prep: 25 mins - **Cook:** 25 mins **Additional:** 20 mins - **Total:** 1 hr 10 mins - **Servings:** 24

INGREDIENTS

- 2 ½ cups all-purpose flour

- ⅓ cup white sugar
- ¼ teaspoon baking powder
- ½ cup shortening
- 2 tablespoons butter
- ½ cup milk
- 1 egg, beaten
- 1 ½ cups dried figs
- ¾ cup golden raisins
- ¼ cup slivered almonds
- ¼ cup white sugar
- ¼ cup hot water
- ¼ teaspoon ground cinnamon
- 1 pinch ground black pepper

DIRECTIONS

Step 1

In a large mixing bowl, combine flour, 1/3 cup sugar and baking powder. Cut in shortening and butter until mixture resembles small peas. Stir in the milk and egg until the dough comes together. Divide dough into two pieces, wrap and refrigerate for about 2 hours or until easy to handle.

Step 2

In a food processor or blender, grind the figs, raisins and almonds until they are coarsely chopped. In a medium bowl, stir together the 1/4 cup of sugar, hot water, cinnamon and pepper. Stir in the fruit mixture, cover and set aside until the dough is ready.

Step 3

Preheat oven to 350 degrees F (175 degrees C).

Step 4

On a lightly floured surface, roll each piece of the dough out to a 12 inch square. Cut each piece into 12 3x4 inch rectangles. Using a heaping tablespoon of filling for each rectangle, spread filling along one of the short sides of the rectangle. Roll up from that side. Place rolls, seam side down, on an ungreased cookie sheet. Curve each roll slightly. Snip outer edge of the curve three times.

Step 5

Bake for 20 to 25 minutes in the preheated oven, until golden brown. Glaze with your favorite confectioners' glaze.

Nutrition Facts

154 calories; protein 2.3g 5% DV; carbohydrates 22.8g 7% DV; fat 6.3g 10% DV; cholesterol 13.2mg 4% DV; sodium 18.3mg 1% DV.

AUNT RITA'S ITALIAN STEW

Prep: 30 mins - **Cook:** 30 mins - **Total:** 1 hr - **Servings:** 6

INGREDIENTS

- 1 pound mild Italian sausage links, cut into 1-inch pieces
- 1 cup chopped onion
- 1 tablespoon minced garlic
- 2 medium (blank)s yellow summer squash, thinly sliced
- 2 eaches zucchini, thinly sliced
- 2 carrot, (7-1/2")s carrots, thinly sliced
- 2 cups sliced fresh mushrooms
- 2 (14.5 ounce) cans Italian-style stewed tomatoes
- 2 tablespoons grated Parmesan cheese

DIRECTIONS

Step 1

Cook the sausage with onion and garlic in a large, deep skillet or pot over medium heat, until the meat is browned, 10 to 15 minutes, stirring frequently. Mix in the summer squash, zucchini, carrots, mushrooms, and stewed tomatoes, reduce heat to medium-low, and bring the mixture to a simmer. Cook, stirring occasionally, until the vegetables are tender, about 20 minutes. Sprinkle with Parmesan cheese, and serve.

Cook's Note

I use my food processor to slice all the vegetables.

Nutrition Facts

Per Serving:

269.9 calories; protein 14.3g 29% DV; carbohydrates 20.7g 7% DV; fat 15.1g 23% DV; cholesterol 31.2mg 10% DV; sodium 967.8mg 39% DV.

POTATO SOUP ITALIAN STYLE

Prep: 10 mins - **Cook:** 25 mins - **Total:** 35 mins - **Servings:** 4

INGREDIENTS

- 3 tablespoons olive oil
- 1 large onion, chopped
- 5 cups water
- 4 medium (2-1/4" to 3" dia, raw)s potatoes, peeled and quartered
- salt and pepper to taste
- 4 large eggs eggs

DIRECTIONS
Step 1

Heat oil in a large pot over medium heat. Saute onions until translucent. To the onions add water, potatoes, salt and pepper. Bring to a boil; reduce heat to low and simmer for 20 minutes, or until potatoes are tender but still firm.

Step 2

Remove from heat and gently crack eggs into soup; be careful not to break eggs. Place on low heat until whites of eggs are cooked. Cool slightly before serving.

Nutrition Facts

342 calories; protein 10.3g 21% DV; carbohydrates 42.2g 14% DV; fat 15.3g 24% DV; cholesterol 186mg 62% DV; sodium 531.4mg 21% DV.

ITALIAN-STYLE BRUSCHETTA

Prep: 15 mins - **Cook:** 5 mins **Additional:** 1 hr - **Total:** 1 hr 20 mins - **Servings:** 8

INGREDIENTS

- 1 ½ pounds plum tomatoes, seeded and cut into small dice
- ¼ cup chopped fresh basil
- 6 tablespoons extra-virgin olive oil, divided
- 2 tablespoons finely chopped red onion
- 2 large cloves garlic, minced
- 2 teaspoons red wine vinegar
- 1 pinch freshly ground black pepper to taste
- 1 French baguette, cut into 1/2-inch thick slices
- 1 tablespoon high-quality balsamic vinegar, or to taste

DIRECTIONS

Step 1

Stir tomatoes, basil, 3 tablespoons olive oil, red onion, garlic, red wine vinegar, and pepper together in a bowl; let tomato mixture stand at room temperature for 15 minutes, then place in the refrigerator to marinate for 45 minutes.

Step 2

Set oven rack about 6 inches from the heat source and preheat the oven's broiler.

Step 3

Brush one side of each slice of bread with remaining olive oil. Place bread slices, oiled-side-up, onto a baking sheet.

Step 4

Broil until golden brown, about 2 minutes; remove from oven. Spoon tomato mixture evenly over the top of toasted bread slices; drizzle balsamic vinegar evenly over tomato mixture. Serve immediately.

Nutrition Facts

234.3 calories; protein 5.9g 12% DV; carbohydrates 28.5g 9% DV; fat 11.1g 17% DV; cholesterolmg; sodium 281.4mg 11% DV.

ALLIGATOR ANIMAL ITALIAN BREAD

Prep: 30 mins - **Cook:** 20 mins **Additional:** 1 hr 10 mins - **Total:** 2 hrs - **Servings:** 8

INGREDIENTS

For the dough:

- 1 cup warm water (110 degrees F/45 degrees C)
- 3 cups all-purpose flour
- 1 tablespoon vital wheat gluten
- 1 ½ teaspoons salt
- 2 ½ teaspoons instant yeast
- For decorating:
- 2 eaches raisins
- 1 egg
- 1 tablespoon water

DIRECTIONS

Step 1

Combine the water, flour, gluten (if using), salt, and yeast in your bread machine and mix using the machine's dough cycle. The dough should pull away from the sides nicely; add more flour or water if necessary during the mixing cycle so the dough doesn't end up too sticky or dry. When the first rising cycle ends, punch the dough down and transfer the dough to a lightly floured surface.

Step 2

Grease a baking sheet or line it with parchment paper. Roll out the dough into a square about 3/4-inch thick and divide it into four pieces. Roll up three of the pieces jelly-roll style, and line them up seam-side down on the baking sheet to form the head, body, and tail. The ends of the connected pieces should just slightly touch. (Remember that everything will get bigger as the dough rises, so try to keep proportions in mind.)

Step 3

Lightly grease your hands and shape the dough like you're working with clay: elongate the tail to a slender curved tip, and then slightly elongate the nose end. Slice into the nose horizontally at the tip to form the alligator's mouth; hold the mouth open with a wedge of greased aluminum foil.

Step 4

From the remaining quarter of dough, trim off a tiny piece to use for the eyes. Slice the remainder into four "logs" for legs, flattening one end of each leg and inserting it under the alligator's body. Shape the legs into slight bends when positioning them on the baking sheet. Cut short slices into the other end of the leg to make claws. Use scissors to snip shallow cuts over the surface of the dough (this will form the alligator's spiky skin). Roll the reserved dough into little balls for the eyes, stuffing each with a raisin.

Step 5

Preheat an oven to 400 degrees F (200 degrees C). Beat the egg with 1 tablespoon of warm water in a small bowl.

Step 6

Let the alligator rise in a warm place until fully proofed, about thirty minutes (poke your index and middle fingers into the sides of the dough; the indentation should remain. If the dough springs back, it needs to rise longer). Gently brush the dough with the egg wash and bake it in the preheated oven until golden brown, about 20 minutes. Remove the alligator from the baking sheet with a spatula and transfer it to a wire rack. Remove the aluminum foil when cool.

Cook's Note

Dried currants or dried cranberry pieces can be substituted for the raisins to form the alligator's eyes.

Nutrition Facts

186.7 calories; protein 6.6g 13% DV; carbohydrates 36.7g 12% DV; fat 1.1g 2% DV; cholesterol 20.5mg 7% DV; sodium 446.2mg 18% DV.

ITALIAN CREAM SODA

Prep: 1 min - **Total:** 1 min - **Servings:** 1

INGREDIENTS

- 8 fluid ounces carbonated water
- ¾ fluid ounce passion fruit flavored syrup
- ¾ fluid ounce watermelon flavored syrup
- 1 fluid ounce half-and-half cream

DIRECTIONS

Step 1

Fill a tall glass half full with ice. Fill to 2/3 with carbonated water. Pour in watermelon and passion fruit flavored syrups, then float the half-and-half cream on top. Stir when ready to drink.

Nutrition Facts

189.9 calories; protein 0.9g 2% DV; carbohydrates 41.8g 14% DV; fat 3.5g 5% DV; cholesterol 11.2mg 4% DV; sodium 46.4mg 2% DV.

ITALIAN SHRIMP CAPRESE PASTA

Prep: 25 mins - **Total:** 25 mins - **Servings:** 4

INGREDIENTS

- 8 ounces uncooked dried linguine
- 2 squares Italian Herb Saute Express® Saute Starter
- 1 pound uncooked medium shrimp, peeled, deveined
- 1 cup grape tomatoes, halved
- 1 cup fresh mozzarella pearls or cubed mozzarella
- ¼ cup chopped fresh basil leaves
- ¼ cup shredded Parmesan cheese

DIRECTIONS

Step 1

Cook pasta according to package directions; drain.

Step 2

Melt Saute Express® squares in 12-inch nonstick skillet over medium-low heat just until bubbles begin to form.

Step 3

Add shrimp.

Step 4

Saute 5-7 minutes or until shrimp turn pink. Add pasta, tomatoes, mozzarella and basil; stir until coated and heated through. Sprinkle with Parmesan cheese.

Nutrition Facts

471 calories; protein 35.1g 70% DV; carbohydrates 44.6g 14% DV; fat 17.4g 27% DV; cholesterol 215.3mg 72% DV; sodium 729.3mg 29% DV.

SPINACH MANICOTTI WITH ITALIAN SAUSAGE

Prep: 15 mins - **Cook:** 1 hr 15 mins - **Total:** 1 hr 30 mins - **Servings:** 6

INGREDIENTS

- 1 (9 ounce) bag fresh spinach
- 1 pound bulk Italian sausage
- 1 (24 ounce) carton small curd cottage cheese
- 1 (12 ounce) package shredded mozzarella cheese, divided
- 12 piece (blank)s manicotti shells
- 2 (24 ounce) jars spaghetti sauce

DIRECTIONS

Step 1

Preheat oven to 350 degrees F (175 degrees C).

Step 2

Bring a pot of water to a boil and immerse spinach in the boiling water until dark green and softened, about 2 minutes. Drain and squeeze out excess moisture.

Step 3

Cook sausage in a skillet over medium heat until browned and crumbly, about 10 minutes, stirring often. Drain excess grease. Combine spinach and sausage in a bowl. Mix cottage cheese and 8 ounces of mozzarella cheese into sausage and spinach, stirring until filling is thoroughly combined.

Step 4

Use your fingers to stuff uncooked manicotti shells with stuffing. Lay stuffed manicotti into a baking dish, side by side, and pour both jars of sauce over manicotti.

Step 5

Bake in the preheated oven until manicotti are tender but still slightly firm to the bite and the filling is hot, 1 hour to 1 hour and 15 minutes. Sprinkle remaining 4 ounces of mozzarella cheese over the dish, let the cheese melt, and serve.

Nutrition Facts

764.7 calories; protein 47.6g 95% DV; carbohydrates 63.5g 21% DV; fat 35.4g 54% DV; cholesterol 87.6mg 29% DV; sodium 2394.7mg 96% DV.

MY BEST CHICKEN PICCATA

Prep: 15 mins - **Cook:** 20 mins - **Total:** 35 mins - **Servings:** 4

INGREDIENTS

- 1 cup all-purpose flour
- 1 teaspoon salt
- ½ teaspoon ground black pepper
- 4 breast half, bone and skin removed (blank)s skinless, boneless chicken breast halves - trimmed and cut in half crosswise
- ½ cup butter
- ¾ cup dry white wine
- 1 lemon, juiced
- 1 teaspoon capers
- 1 lemon, sliced
- 2 teaspoons chopped fresh parsley

DIRECTIONS

Step 1

Mix flour, salt, and black pepper in a bowl. Dredge the chicken breast pieces in the seasoned flour to coat;

tap off excess flour.

Step 2

Melt butter in a skillet over medium heat until hot but not starting to brown. Pan-fry coated chicken breast pieces in the hot butter until golden brown, the juices run clear, and the chicken is no longer pink inside, about 10 minutes. Turn the chicken pieces often. Remove chicken from skillet and keep warm.

Step 3

Pour white wine into the skillet and scrape pan to dissolve any browned bits of food on the bottom. Mix in lemon juice, reduce heat to low, and simmer until sauce is slightly thickened, about 10 minutes. Stir often. Stir capers into sauce and place chicken back into skillet, turning to coat with sauce.

Step 4

To serve, transfer chicken to a serving platter, top with sauce, and garnish with lemon slices and fresh parsley.

Nutrition Facts

484.4 calories; protein 26.8g 54% DV; carbohydrates 29.3g 9% DV; fat 25.8g 40% DV; cholesterol 121.8mg 41% DV; sodium 820.2mg 33% DV.

ITALIAN SAUSAGE TORTELLINI SOUP

Prep: 15 mins - **Cook**: 55 mins - **Total**: 1 hr 10 mins - **Servings**: 6

INGREDIENTS

- 1 (3.5 ounce) link sweet Italian sausage, casings removed
- 1 cup chopped onions
- 2 cloves garlic, minced
- 5 cups beef stock
- ⅓ cup water
- ½ cup red wine
- 4 medium whole (2-3/5" dia) (blank)s tomatoes - peeled, seeded and chopped
- 1 cup chopped carrots
- ½ teaspoon dried basil
- ½ teaspoon dried oregano
- 1 cup tomato sauce
- 1 zucchini, chopped
- 8 ounces cheese tortellini
- 1 green bell pepper, chopped
- 1 tablespoon chopped fresh parsley
- 2 tablespoons grated Parmesan cheese for topping

DIRECTIONS

Step 1

Place the sausage in a large pot over medium high heat and saute for 10 minutes, or until well browned. Drain the fat except for about 1 tablespoon, add the onions and garlic and saute for 5 more minutes.

Step 2

Next add the beef stock, water, wine, tomatoes, carrots, basil, oregano and tomato sauce. Bring to a boil, reduce heat to low and simmer for 30 minutes, skimming any fat that may surface.

Step 3

Add the zucchini, tortellini, green bell pepper and parsley to taste. Simmer for 10 minutes, or until tortellini is fully Cooked. Pour into individual bowls and garnish with the cheese.

Nutrition Facts

249.4 calories; protein 12.4g 25% DV; carbohydrates 27.7g 9% DV; fat 8.9g 14% DV; cholesterol 21.7mg 7% DV; sodium 541.8mg 22% DV.

BEST ITALIAN SAUSAGE SOUP

Prep: 15 mins - **Cook**: 55 mins - **Total**: 1 hr 10 mins - **Servings**: 6

INGREDIENTS

- 1 ½ pounds sweet Italian sausage
- 2 cloves garlic, minced
- 2 small onions, chopped
- 2 (16 ounce) cans whole peeled tomatoes
- 1 ¼ cups dry red wine
- 5 cups beef broth
- ½ teaspoon dried basil
- ½ teaspoon dried oregano
- 2 medium (blank)s zucchini, sliced
- 1 green bell pepper, chopped
- 3 tablespoons chopped fresh parsley
- 1 (16 ounce) package spinach fettuccine pasta
- salt and pepper to taste

DIRECTIONS

Instructions Checklist

Step 1

In a large pot, Cook sausage over medium heat until brown. Remove with a slotted spoon, and drain on paper towels. Drain fat from pan, reserving 3 tablespoons.

Step 2

Cook garlic and onion in reserved fat for 2 to 3 minutes. Stir in tomatoes, wine, broth, basil, and oregano. Transfer to a slow Cooker, and stir in sausage, zucchini, bell pepper, and parsley.

Step 3

Cover, and Cook on Low for 4 to 6 hours.

Step 4

Bring a pot of lightly salted water to a boil. Cook pasta in boiling water until al dente, about 7 minutes. Drain water, and add pasta to the slow Cooker. Simmer for a few minutes, and season with salt and pepper before serving.

Nutrition Facts

436.2 calories; protein 21g 42% DV; carbohydrates 43.5g 14% DV; fat 17.8g 27% DV; cholesterol 33.4mg 11% DV; sodium 1609.2mg 64% DV.

ITALIAN SAUSAGE SOUP

Prep: 10 mins - **Cook:** 40 mins - **Total:** 50 mins - **Servings:** 6

INGREDIENTS

- 1 pound Italian sausage
- 1 clove garlic, minced
- 2 (14 ounce) cans beef broth
- 1 (14.5 ounce) can Italian-style stewed tomatoes
- 1 cup sliced carrots
- 1 (14.5 ounce) can great Northern beans, undrained
- 2 small zucchini, cubed
- 2 cups spinach - packed, rinsed and torn
- ¼ teaspoon ground black pepper
- ¼ teaspoon salt

DIRECTIONS

Step 1

In a stockpot or Dutch oven, brown sausage with garlic. Stir in broth, tomatoes and carrots, and season with salt and pepper. Reduce heat, cover, and simmer 15 minutes.

Step 2

Stir in beans with liquid and zucchini. Cover, and simmer another 15 minutes, or until zucchini is tender.

Step 3

Remove from heat, and add spinach. Replace lid allowing the heat from the soup to Cook the spinach leaves. Soup is ready to serve after 5 minutes.

Nutrition Facts

385.4 calories; protein 18.8g 38% DV; carbohydrates 22.5g 7% DV; fat 24.4g 38% DV; cholesterol 57.5mg

19% DV; sodium 1258.7mg 50% DV.

MANICOTTI ITALIAN CASSEROLE

Prep: 10 mins - **Cook:** 30 mins - **Total:** 40 mins - **Servings:** 8

INGREDIENTS

- 1 pound rigatoni pasta
- 1 pound ground beef
- 1 pound Italian sausage
- 1 (8 ounce) can mushrooms, drained
- 2 (32 ounce) jars spaghetti sauce
- 1 ½ pounds shredded mozzarella cheese
- 1 (3 ounce) package thinly sliced pepperoni

DIRECTIONS

Step 1

Preheat oven to 350 degrees F (175 degrees C).

Step 2

Bring a large pot of lightly salted water to boil. Pour in rigatoni, and Cook until al dente, about 8 to 10 minutes. Drain, and set pasta aside.

Step 3

Meanwhile, brown ground beef and italian sausage in a large skillet over medium heat. With a slotted spoon, remove beef and sausage to a baking dish. Stir mushrooms, spaghetti sauce, and Cooked pasta into the baking dish. Sprinkle cheese and pepperoni over the top.

Step 4

Bake in preheated oven until the cheese is brown and bubbly, about 20 minutes.

Nutrition Facts

909 calories; protein 52.1g 104% DV; carbohydrates 77.6g 25% DV; fat 43g 66% DV; cholesterol 126.8mg 42% DV; sodium 2247.8mg 90% DV.

ITALIAN MEATBALLS

Prep: 20 mins - **Cook:** 35 mins **Additional:** 1 hr 20 mins - **Total:** 2 hrs 15 mins - **Servings:** 30

INGREDIENTS

- ⅓ cup plain bread crumbs
- ½ cup milk
- 2 tablespoons olive oil
- 1 onion, diced

- 1 pound ground beef
- 1 pound ground pork
- 2 large eggs eggs
- ¼ bunch fresh parsley, chopped
- 3 cloves garlic, crushed
- 2 teaspoons salt
- 1 teaspoon ground black pepper
- ½ teaspoon red pepper flakes
- 1 teaspoon dried Italian herb seasoning
- 2 tablespoons grated Parmesan cheese

DIRECTIONS

Step 1

Cover a baking sheet with foil and spray lightly with Cooking spray.

Step 2

Soak bread crumbs in milk in a small bowl for 20 minutes.

Step 3

Heat olive oil in a skillet over medium heat. Cook and stir onions in hot oil until translucent, about 20 minutes.

Step 4

Mix beef and pork together in a large bowl. Stir onions, bread crumb mixture, eggs, parsley, garlic, salt, black pepper, red pepper flakes, Italian herb seasoning, and Parmesan cheese into meat mixture with a rubber spatula until combined. Cover and refrigerate for about one hour.

Step 5

Preheat an oven to 425 degrees F (220 degrees C).

Step 6

Using wet hands, form meat mixture into balls about 1 1/2 inches in diameter. Arrange onto **prep**ared baking sheet.

Step 7

Bake in the preheated oven until browned and Cooked through, 15 to 20 minutes.

Cook's Notes:

Some recipes use equal portions of beef, veal, and pork, which is also nice, yet more expensive. These days you can find all sorts of lean-to-fat ratios for ground beef. Most stores sell 90% lean, 10% fat, but I prefer the 80% lean, 20% fat ratio for this recipe.

Once Cooked, you can add the meatballs to your favorite prepared tomato sauce for 1 to 2 hours.

Nutrition Facts

81.9 calories; protein 6.2g 12% DV; carbohydrates 1.7g 1% DV; fat 5.5g 8% DV; cholesterol 32.3mg 11% DV; sodium 192.1mg 8% DV.

BAKED PENNE WITH ITALIAN SAUSAGE

Prep: 15 mins - **Cook:** 35 mins - **Total:** 50 mins - **Servings:** 6
INGREDIENTS

- 1 (12 ounce) package dry penne pasta
- 2 teaspoons olive oil
- 1 pound mild Italian sausage
- 1 cup chopped onion
- ½ cup white wine
- 1 (15 ounce) can tomato sauce
- 1 (14.5 ounce) can diced tomatoes with garlic
- 1 (6 ounce) can tomato paste

2 cups shredded mozzarella cheese

DIRECTIONS

Step 1

Preheat oven to 350 degrees F (175 degrees C). Bring a large pot of lightly salted water to a boil. Add pasta and Cook for 8 to 10 minutes or until al dente; drain.

Step 2

Heat oil in a large, deep skillet. Place sausage and onion in the skillet and Cook over medium high heat until evenly brown. Drain excess fat. Pour in wine, and Cook for 1 minute, stirring, to deglaze the pan. Stir in tomato sauce, diced tomatoes and tomato paste. Simmer for 10 minutes, stirring occasionally. Toss with Cooked pasta, and place in a 9x13 inch baking dish. Sprinkle top with mozzarella.

Step 3

Bake in preheated oven for 20 minutes, or until cheese is melted.

Nutrition Facts

664.1 calories; protein 31g 62% DV; carbohydrates 59.2g 19% DV; fat 33.5g 52% DV; cholesterol 81.6mg 27% DV; sodium 1714.1mg 69% DV.

ITALIAN POPCORN WITH PARMESAN

Prep: 10 mins - **Cook:** 5 mins - **Total:** 15 mins - **Servings:** 6
INGREDIENTS

- 6 tablespoons unpopped popcorn
- ¼ cup olive oil
- 2 tablespoons olive oil
- 1 ½ tablespoons Italian seasoning

- 1 ½ teaspoons garlic salt
- 1 cup freshly grated Parmigiano cheese

DIRECTIONS

Step 1

Combine popcorn and 1/4 cup olive oil in a 2-quart saucepan; cover. Cook over high heat, continuously shaking the pan, until the popcorn is popped and the lid begins to lift from the popcorn, about 5 minutes. Pour popcorn into a large bowl.

Step 2

Mix 2 tablespoons olive oil, Italian seasoning, and garlic salt into popcorn; toss to coat. Add Parmesan cheese and mix well.

Cook's Note:

For best results, use freshly ground Italian seasoning and garlic salt. Adjust salt according to taste.

Nutrition Facts

227.3 calories; protein 6.8g 14% DV; carbohydrates 10.6g 3% DV; fat 18g 28% DV; cholesterol 11.7mg 4% DV; sodium 657.7mg 26% DV.

ITALIAN VEGETABLE SOUP

Prep: 20 mins - **Cook:** 50 mins - **Total:** 1 hr 10 mins - **Servings:** 8

INGREDIENTS

- 1 pound ground beef
- 1 cup chopped onion
- 1 cup chopped celery
- 1 cup chopped carrots
- 2 cloves garlic, minced
- 1 (14.5 ounce) can peeled and diced tomatoes
- 1 (15 ounce) can tomato sauce
- 2 (19 ounce) cans kidney beans, drained and rinsed
- 2 cups water
- 5 teaspoons beef bouillon granules
- 1 tablespoon dried parsley
- ½ teaspoon dried oregano
- ½ teaspoon dried basil
- 2 cups chopped cabbage
- 1 (15.25 ounce) can whole kernel corn
- 1 (15 ounce) can green beans

- 1 cup macaroni

DIRECTIONS

Step 1

Place ground beef in a large soup pot. Cook over medium heat until evenly browned. Drain excess fat. Stir in onion, celery, carrots, garlic, chopped tomatoes, tomato sauce, beans, water and bouillon. Season with parsley, oregano and basil. Simmer for 20 minutes.

Step 2

Stir in cabbage, corn, green beans and pasta. Bring to a boil, then reduce heat. Simmer until vegetables are tender and pasta is al dente. Add more water if needed.

Nutrition Facts

440.7 calories; protein 22.4g 45% DV; carbohydrates 52.5g 17% DV; fat 16.6g 26% DV; cholesterol 48.4mg 16% DV; sodium 1295mg 52% DV.

ITALIAN HERB BREAD

Prep: 30 mins - **Cook:** 35 mins **Additional:** 1 hr 35 mins - **Total:** 2 hrs 40 mins - **Servings:** 24

INGREDIENTS

- 2 (.25 ounce) packages active dry yeast
- 2 cups warm water (110 degrees F/45 degrees C)
- 2 tablespoons white sugar
- ¼ cup olive oil
- 1 tablespoon salt
- 1 tablespoon dried basil
- 1 tablespoon dried oregano
- 1 teaspoon garlic powder
- 1 teaspoon onion powder
- ½ cup grated Romano cheese
- 6 cups bread flour

DIRECTIONS

Step 1

Mix yeast, warm water, and white sugar together in a large bowl. Set aside for five minutes, or until mixture becomes foamy.

Step 2

Stir olive oil, salt, herbs, garlic powder, onion powder, cheese, and 3 cups flour into the yeast mixture. Gradually mix in the next three cups of flour. Dough will be stiff.

Step 3

Knead dough for 5 to 10 minutes, or until it is smooth and rubbery. Place in an oiled bowl, and turn to cover the surface of the dough with oil. Cover with a damp linen dish towel. Allow to rise for one hour, or until the dough has doubled in size.

Step 4

Punch dough down to release all the air. Shape into two loaves. Place loaves on a greased Cookie sheet, or into two greased 9 x 5 inch loaf pans. Allow to rise until doubled in size, about a 30 minutes.

Step 5

Bake at 350 degrees F (175 degrees C) for 35 minutes. Remove loaves from pan(s), and let cool on wire racks for at least 15 minutes before slicing.

Nutrition Facts

37 calories; protein 1.1g 2% DV; carbohydrates 1.7g 1% DV; fat 3g 5% DV; cholesterol 2.6mg 1% DV; sodium 320.9mg 13% DV.

HOT ITALIAN GIARDINIERA

Prep: 45 mins - **Cook:** 2 days - **Total:** 2 days - **Servings:** 10

INGREDIENTS

- 2 medium (blank)s green bell peppers, diced
- 2 medium (blank)s red bell peppers, diced
- 8 peppers fresh jalapeno peppers, sliced
- 1 celery stalk, diced
- 1 medium carrot, diced
- 1 small onion, chopped
- ½ cup fresh cauliflower florets
- ½ cup salt
- 2 cups water to cover
- 2 cloves garlic, finely chopped
- 1 tablespoon dried oregano
- 1 teaspoon red pepper flakes
- ½ teaspoon black pepper
- 1 (5 ounce) jar pimento-stuffed green olives, chopped
- 1 cup white vinegar
- 1 cup olive oil

DIRECTIONS

Step 1

Place into a bowl the green and red peppers, jalapenos, celery, carrots, onion, and cauliflower. Stir in salt, and fill with enough cold water to cover. Place plastic wrap or aluminum foil over the bowl, and refrigerate overnight.

Step 2

The next day, drain salty water, and rinse vegetables. In a bowl, mix together garlic, oregano, red pepper flakes, black pepper, and olives. Pour in vinegar and olive oil, and mix well. Combine with vegetable mixture, cover, and refrigerate for 2 days before using.

Editor's Note:

Nutrition data for this recipe includes the full amount of brine ingredients. The actual amount of brine consumed will vary.

Nutrition Facts

232.7 calories; protein 1.2g 2% DV; carbohydrates 5.9g 2% DV; fat 23.5g 36% DV; cholesterolmg; sodium 305.9mg 12% DV.

ITALIAN SPAGHETTI SAUCE WITH MEATBALLS

Prep: 20 mins - **Cook:** 2 hrs - **Total:** 2 hrs 20 mins - **Servings:** 6

INGREDIENTS

Meatballs

- 1 pound lean ground beef
- 1 cup fresh bread crumbs
- 1 tablespoon dried parsley
- 1 tablespoon grated Parmesan cheese
- ¼ teaspoon ground black pepper
- ⅛ teaspoon garlic powder
- 1 egg, beaten

Sauce

- ¾ cup chopped onion
- 5 cloves garlic, minced
- ¼ cup olive oil
- 2 (28 ounce) cans whole peeled tomatoes
- 2 teaspoons salt
- 1 teaspoon white sugar
- 1 bay leaf
- 1 (6 ounce) can tomato paste
- ¾ teaspoon dried basil
- ½ teaspoon ground black pepper

DIRECTIONS
Step 1
In a large bowl, combine ground beef, bread crumbs, parsley, Parmesan, 1/4 teaspoon black pepper, garlic powder and beaten egg. Mix well and form into 12 balls. Store, covered, in refrigerator until needed.
Step 2
In a large saucepan over medium heat, saute onion and garlic in olive oil until onion is translucent. Stir in tomatoes, salt, sugar and bay leaf. Cover, reduce heat to low, and simmer 90 minutes. Stir in tomato paste, basil, 1/2 teaspoon pepper and meatballs and simmer 30 minutes more. Serve.
Nutrition Facts
346.6 calories; protein 18.9g 38% DV; carbohydrates 23g 7% DV; fat 21.2g 33% DV; cholesterol 77.4mg 26% DV; sodium 1492.5mg 60% DV.

ITALIAN SAUSAGE SOUP

Prep: 15 mins - **Cook:** 1 hr - **Total:** 1 hr 15 mins - **Servings:** 8
INGREDIENTS
- 2 tablespoons olive oil
- 1 pound Italian sausage, casings removed
- 1 ½ cups chopped onion
- 1 ½ cups sliced carrots
- 1 stalk celery with leaves, chopped
- 1 tablespoon chopped garlic
- 1 teaspoon dried basil
- 1 teaspoon dried rosemary
- ¼ teaspoon dried crushed red pepper
- ¼ teaspoon dried sage
- 1 (14.5 ounce) can canned diced tomatoes
- 5 cups chicken broth
- 1 (16 ounce) can kidney beans, drained
- 1 cup unCooked pasta shells

DIRECTIONS
Step 1
Heat the oil in a large pot over medium-high heat. Cook the sausage until evenly browned, and break into pieces. Stir in the onions, carrots, celery, garlic, basil, rosemary, red pepper, and sage. Continue Cooking 10 minutes, until vegetables are tender. Mix in tomatoes, and Cook until heated through. Stir in the broth and beans. Bring to a boil. Reduce heat to low, and simmer 20 minutes.

Step 2

Stir pasta into soup, and continue Cooking 10 minutes, or until pasta is al dente.

Nutrition Facts

364.7 calories; protein 14.2g 29% DV; carbohydrates 27.3g 9% DV; fat 21.8g 34% DV; cholesterol 43.1mg 14% DV; sodium 636.9mg 26% DV.

ITALIAN PORK TENDERLOIN

Prep: 15 mins - **Cook:** 35 mins - **Total:** 50 mins - **Servings:** 4

INGREDIENTS

- 2 tablespoons olive oil
- ¼ cup chopped prosciutto
- 2 tablespoons chopped fresh sage
- 2 tablespoons chopped fresh parsley
- 2 tablespoons chopped oil-packed sun-dried tomatoes
- ¼ cup chopped onion
- 1 ½ pounds pork tenderloin, cut into 1/2 inch strips
- ½ cup chicken broth
- ½ cup heavy cream
- ¼ teaspoon salt
- ½ teaspoon ground black pepper

DIRECTIONS

Step 1

Heat the oil in a skillet over medium-high heat. Saute the prosciutto, sage, parsley, sun-dried tomatoes, and onion 5 minutes, until onion is tender. Mix the pork strips into the skillet, and brown about 10 minutes, turning once.

Step 2

Stir the broth and heavy cream into the skillet, and season with salt and pepper. Bring to a boil. Reduce heat to low, and simmer 20 minutes, stirring occasionally, until pork reaches a minimum temperature of 145 degrees F (63 degrees C) and sauce is thickened.

Nutrition Facts

356 calories; protein 28.9g 58% DV; carbohydrates 3.1g 1% DV; fat 25g 39% DV; cholesterol 121.8mg 41% DV; sodium 390.3mg 16% DV.

CREAMY ITALIAN DRESSING

Prep: 10 mins - **Total:** 10 mins - **Servings:** 12

INGREDIENTS

- 1 cup mayonnaise
- ½ small onion
- 2 tablespoons red wine vinegar
- 1 tablespoon white sugar
- ¾ teaspoon Italian seasoning
- ¼ teaspoon garlic powder
- ¼ teaspoon salt
- ⅛ teaspoon ground black pepper

DIRECTIONS

Step 1

In a blender or food processor, combine mayonnaise, onion, vinegar, and sugar. Season with Italian seasoning, garlic powder, salt, and pepper. Blend until smooth.

Nutrition Facts

139 calories; protein 0.2g 1% DV; carbohydrates 2.4g 1% DV; fat 14.6g 22% DV; cholesterol 7mg 2% DV; sodium 153mg 6% DV.

ITALIAN CREAM CAKE II

Servings: 10

INGREDIENTS

- ½ cup margarine, softened
- ½ cup shortening
- 2 cups white sugar
- 5 large egg yolks egg yolks
- 2 cups all-purpose flour
- 1 teaspoon baking soda
- 1 cup buttermilk
- 1 teaspoon vanilla extract
- 1 ⅓ cups flaked coconut
- 1 cup chopped pecans
- 5 large egg whites egg whites
- 8 ounces cream cheese
- ½ cup margarine, softened
- 4 cups confectioners' sugar
- 1 teaspoon vanilla extract

- ½ cup chopped pecans

DIRECTIONS

Step 1

Preheat oven to 350 degrees F (175 degrees C). Grease and flour three 8 inch round cake pans.

Step 2

Beat egg whites until they form stiff peaks.

Step 3

In a large bowl, cream 1/2 cup margarine and shortening till light. Add white sugar, and beat till fluffy. Beat in egg yolks. Stir together flour and baking soda, and add alternately with buttermilk into the creamed mixture; mix well after each addition. Stir in 1 teaspoon vanilla, coconut, and 1 cup pecans. Fold in stiffly beaten egg whites. Spoon into prepared pans.

Step 4

Bake for 25 to 40 minutes. Cool in pans for 10 minutes. Remove to wire rack to cool completely.

Step 5

Combine cream cheese, 1/2 cup margarine, confectioners' sugar, and 1 teaspoon vanilla in mixer bowl. Beat till smooth. Add coconut if desired. Frost the cooled cake. The remaining 1/2 cup pecans can be stirred into frosting or sprinkled onto the cake after it is frosted.

Nutrition Facts

967.2 calories; protein 10.3g 21% DV; carbohydrates 116.8g 38% DV; fat 53.3g 82% DV; cholesterol 128.4mg 43% DV; sodium 489.9mg 20% DV.

ITALIAN GRILLED CHEESE SANDWICHES

Prep: 8 mins - **Cook**: 7 mins - **Total**: 15 mins - **Servings**: 6

INGREDIENTS

- ¼ cup unsalted butter
- ⅛ teaspoon garlic powder
- 12 slices white bread
- 1 teaspoon dried oregano
- 1 (8 ounce) package shredded mozzarella cheese
- 1 (24 ounce) jar vodka marinara sauce

DIRECTIONS

Step 1

Preheat your oven's broiler.

Step 2

Place 6 slices of bread onto a baking sheet. Spread a small handful of the mozzarella cheese over each slice. Top with the remaining 6 slices of bread. Mix together the butter and garlic powder, brush some over the tops of the sandwiches, or spread with the back of a tablespoon. Sprinkle with dried oregano.

Step 3

Place baking sheet under the broiler for 2 to 3 minutes, until golden brown. Remove pan from oven, flip sandwiches, and brush the other sides with butter, and sprinkle with oregano. Return to the broiler, and Cook until golden, about 2 minutes.

Step 4

Cut sandwiches in half diagonally, and serve immediately with vodka sauce on the side for dipping.

Nutrition Facts

394 calories; protein 15g 30% DV; carbohydrates 42g 14% DV; fat 18.3g 28% DV; cholesterol 46.5mg 16% DV; sodium 1031.9mg 41% DV.

CALIFORNIA ITALIAN WEDDING SOUP

Prep: 10 mins - **Cook:** 15 mins - **Total:** 25 mins - **Servings:**6

INGREDIENTS

- ½ pound extra-lean ground beef
- 1 egg, lightly beaten
- 2 tablespoons Italian-seasoned breadcrumbs
- 1 tablespoon grated Parmesan cheese
- 2 tablespoons shredded fresh basil leaves
- 1 tablespoon chopped Italian flat leaf parsley
- 2 medium (4-1/8" long)s green onions, sliced
- 5 ¾ cups chicken broth
- 2 cups finely sliced escarole (spinach may be substituted)
- 1 lemon, zested
- ½ cup orzo (rice-shaped pasta), unCooked
- 1 tablespoon grated Parmesan cheese for topping

DIRECTIONS

Step 1

Mix together the meat, egg, bread crumbs, cheese, basil, parsley, and green onions; shape into 3/4 inch balls.

Step 2

Pour broth into a large saucepan over high heat. When boiling, drop in meatballs. Stir in escarole, lemon zest and orzo. Return to a boil; reduce heat to medium. Cook at a slow boil for 10 minutes or until orzo is tender, stirring frequently. Serve sprinkled with cheese.

Nutrition Facts

158.9 calories; protein 11.5g 23% DV; carbohydrates 15.4g 5% DV; fat 5.6g 9% DV; cholesterol 55.3mg 18% DV; sodium 98.6mg 4% DV.

ITALIAN SUBS - RESTAURANT STYLE

Prep: 20 mins Additional: 1 hr - **Total:** 1 hr 20 mins - **Servings:** 8

INGREDIENTS

- 1 head red leaf lettuce, rinsed and torn
- 2 medium fresh tomatoes, chopped
- 1 medium red onion, chopped
- 6 tablespoons olive oil
- 2 tablespoons white wine vinegar
- 2 tablespoons chopped fresh parsley
- 2 cloves garlic, chopped
- 1 teaspoon dried basil
- ¼ teaspoon red pepper flakes
- 1 pinch dried oregano
- ½ pound sliced Capacola sausage
- ½ pound thinly sliced Genoa salami
- ¼ pound thinly sliced prosciutto
- ½ pound sliced provolone cheese
- 4 eaches submarine rolls, split
- 1 cup dill pickle slices

DIRECTIONS

Step 1

In a large bowl, toss together the lettuce, tomatoes and onion. In a separate bowl, whisk together the olive oil, white wine vinegar, parsley, garlic, basil, red pepper flakes and oregano. Pour over the salad, and toss to coat evenly. Refrigerate for about 1 hour.

Step 2

Spread the submarine rolls open, and layer the Capacola, salami, prosciutto, and provolone cheese evenly on each roll. Top with some of the salad, and as many pickle slices as desired. Close the rolls and serve.

Nutrition Facts

707.7 calories; protein 29.2g 58% DV; carbohydrates 40.4g 13% DV; fat 47.3g 73% DV; cholesterol 78.9mg 26% DV; sodium 2083mg 83% DV.

ITALIAN CREME LAYER CAKE

Prep: 30 mins - **Cook:** 30 mins **Additional:** 30 mins - **Total:** 1 hr 30 mins - **Servings:** 12

INGREDIENTS

- 1 cup buttermilk
- 1 teaspoon baking soda
- 2 cups white sugar
- ½ cup butter
- ½ cup vegetable oil
- ½ cup shortening
- 4 large egg yolks egg yolks
- 1 teaspoon vanilla extract
- 4 large egg whites egg whites
- 2 cups all-purpose flour
- 1 (3.5 ounce) package flaked coconut
- 1 cup chopped pecans
- 1 (8 ounce) package cream cheese, softened
- ½ cup margarine, softened
- 4 cups confectioners' sugar
- 1 teaspoon vanilla extract
- 1 cup chopped pecans

DIRECTIONS

Step 1

Preheat oven to 325 degrees F (165 degrees C). Grease three 9 inch, round cake pans. Combine soda and buttermilk, and let stand a few minutes.

Step 2

In a large bowl, cream sugar, 1/2 cup butter, 1/2 cup oil and shortening. Add egg yolks one at a time, beating well after each addition. Mix buttermilk mixture alternately with flour into creamed mixture. Stir in 1 teaspoon vanilla.

Step 3

In a large glass or metal mixing bowl, beat egg whites until stiff peaks form. Fold 1/3 of the whites into the batter, then quickly fold in remaining whites until no streaks remain. Gently stir in 1 cup pecans and coconut.

Step 4

Pour batter into prepared pans. Bake in the preheated oven for 25 to 30 minutes, or until a toothpick inserted into the center of the cake comes out clean. Allow to cool.

Step 5

To make the Cream Cheese Frosting: Beat together cream cheese, 1/2 cup butter or margarine, 1 teaspoon vanilla, and confectioners' sugar. Stir in 1 cup chopped pecans. Frost and fill cooled cake with cream cheese frosting.

Nutrition Facts

924.6 calories; protein 8.5g 17% DV; carbohydrates 99.1g 32% DV; fat 57.4g 88% DV; cholesterol 110mg 37% DV; sodium 376.4mg 15% DV.

HEARTY ITALIAN MEATBALL SOUP

Prep: 10 mins - **Cook:** 20 mins - **Total:** 30 mins - **Servings:** 8

INGREDIENTS

- 3 cups water
- 2 (14 ounce) cans diced tomatoes with onion and garlic, undrained
- 2 (14 ounce) cans beef broth
- 1 teaspoon Italian seasoning
- 1 (16 ounce) package frozen Cooked Italian-style meatballs
- 2 cups frozen Italian-blend vegetables
- 1 cup small star-shaped dried pasta
- ¼ cup grated Parmesan cheese

DIRECTIONS

Step 1

Stir water, tomatoes, beef broth, and Italian seasoning together in a large pot; bring to a boil. Add meatballs, Italian-blend vegetables, and pasta to the pot. Return broth to a boil, reduce heat to medium-low, and Cook until the meatballs are heated through and the pasta is tender, about 10 minutes. Ladle soup into bowls and garnish with Parmesan cheese.

Nutrition Facts

Per Serving:

271.6 calories; protein 16.7g 33% DV; carbohydrates 30.8g 10% DV; fat 8.9g 14% DV; cholesterol 49.3mg 16% DV; sodium 498.1mg 20% DV.

TENDER ITALIAN BAKED CHICKEN

Prep: 10 mins - **Cook:** 20 mins - **Total:** 30 mins - **Servings:** 4

INGREDIENTS

- ¾ cup mayonnaise
- ½ cup grated Parmesan cheese
- ¾ teaspoon garlic powder
- ¾ cup Italian seasoned bread crumbs
- 4 breast half, bone and skin removed (blank)s skinless, boneless chicken breast halves

DIRECTIONS

Step 1

Preheat oven to 425 degrees F (220 degrees C).

Step 2

In a bowl, mix the mayonnaise, Parmesan cheese, and garlic powder. Place bread crumbs in a separate bowl. Dip chicken into the mayonnaise mixture, then into the bread crumbs to coat. Arrange coated chicken on a baking sheet.

Step 3

Bake 20 minutes in the preheated oven, or until chicken juices run clear and coating is golden brown.

Nutrition Facts

553.9 calories; protein 31.8g 64% DV; carbohydrates 17.1g 6% DV; fat 39.6g 61% DV; cholesterol 91.6mg 31% DV; sodium 768.3mg 31% DV.

ITALIAN WEDDING CAKE

Prep: 1 hr - **Cook:** 35 mins - **Total:** 1 hr 35 mins - **Servings:** 10

INGREDIENTS

- ½ cup buttermilk
- 1 teaspoon baking soda
- 1 teaspoon salt
- ½ cup shortening
- ½ cup margarine
- 2 cups white sugar
- 5 large egg yolks egg yolks
- ¼ teaspoon almond extract
- 1 teaspoon vanilla extract
- 2 cups all-purpose flour
- 5 large egg whites egg whites
- ½ cup drained crushed pineapple
- ½ cup flaked coconut
- 1 cup chopped pecans
- ¾ cup butter, softened
- 1 (8 ounce) package cream cheese, softened
- 4 cups confectioners' sugar
- 2 teaspoons vanilla extract
- 1 cup chopped pecans

DIRECTIONS

Step 1

Preheat oven to 350 degrees F (175 degrees C). Grease and flour three 8 inch pans. Combine the buttermilk, baking soda and salt. Set aside.

Step 2

In a large bowl, cream together the shortening, margarine and sugar until light and fluffy. Beat in the egg yolks one at a time, then stir in 1 teaspoon vanilla and almond extract. Beat in the buttermilk mixture alternately with the flour, mixing just until incorporated. In a separate bowl, beat the egg whites until they form stiff peaks. Gently fold the egg whites into the batter. Stir in pineapple, coconut and 1 cup pecans.

Step 3

Pour batter evenly into prepared pans. Bake in the preheated oven for 35 minutes, or until a toothpick inserted into the center of the cake comes out clean. Allow cake layers to cool 10 minutes in pans, then turn out onto wire racks to cool completely.

Step 4

To make the frosting: Cream together the butter, cream cheese and confectioners' sugar until blended. Stir in 2 teaspoons vanilla and 1 cup pecans. If frosting is too stiff to spread, stir in milk a teaspoon at a time until it reaches desired consistency.

Nutrition Facts

1043.7 calories; protein 10.4g 21% DV; carbohydrates 118g 38% DV; fat 61.6g 95% DV; cholesterol 164.2mg 55% DV; sodium 684.3mg 27% DV.

MEXI-ITALIAN SALSA

Prep: 25 mins - **Total**: 25 mins - **Servings**: 10

INGREDIENTS

- 3 plum tomato (blank)s roma (plum) tomatoes, chopped
- ½ onion, chopped
- 1 (2.25 ounce) can sliced black olives, drained
- 1 (6 ounce) can marinated artichoke hearts, drained and chopped
- 2 tablespoons lemon juice
- 2 cloves garlic, minced
- 3 tablespoons chopped fresh basil
- ¼ teaspoon crushed red pepper flakes
- ¼ teaspoon Italian seasoning
- ¼ teaspoon ground cumin
- 3 tablespoons chopped fresh cilantro
- ¼ teaspoon salt
- ⅛ teaspoon ground black pepper

DIRECTIONS

Step 1

Gently stir the tomatoes, onion, olives, and artichoke hearts in a bowl; set aside. Whisk together the lemon juice, garlic, basil, red pepper flakes, Italian seasoning, cumin, cilantro, salt, and pepper in a separate bowl. Fold the dressing into the tomato mixture.

Nutrition Facts

30.4 calories; protein 1g 2% DV; carbohydrates 4.1g 1% DV; fat 1.7g 3% DV; cholesterolmg; sodium 177.9mg 7% DV.

CHOCOLATE ITALIAN CREAM CAKE

Servings: 10

INGREDIENTS

- ½ cup butter
- ½ cup shortening
- 2 cups white sugar
- 5 large eggs eggs
- 2 cups all-purpose flour
- 1 teaspoon baking soda
- ¼ cup unsweetened cocoa powder
- 1 cup buttermilk
- 1 teaspoon vanilla extract
- 1 cup shredded coconut
- 1 cup chopped pecans
- 1 cup cream cheese
- ½ cup butter
- ¼ cup unsweetened cocoa powder
- 4 cups sifted confectioners' sugar
- 1 cup chopped pecans
- 1 teaspoon vanilla extract

DIRECTIONS

Step 1

Preheat oven to 325 degrees F (165 degrees C). Grease and flour three 8-inch round cake pans. Separate the eggs.

Step 2

Cream 1/2 cup of the butter, shortening and sugar together. Add egg yolks, one at a time, beating after each addition. Stir in 1 teaspoon of the vanilla.

Step 3

Sift soda, flour and 1/4 cup cocoa together. Add alternately with buttermilk to the creamed mixture, beginning and ending with dry ingredients. Stir in the coconut and 1 cup of the chopped pecans.

Step 4

Beat the egg whites until stiff peaks form and fold into the batter. Pour batter into the prepared cake pans.

Step 5

Bake at 325 degrees F (165 degrees C) for 25 to 30 minutes. Let cakes cool completely before frosting between layers and on sides.

Step 6

To Make Frosting: Cream the cream cheese and butter together. Sift confectioner's sugar and 1/4 cup cocoa, beating in a little at a time until well-creamed. Add 1 teaspoon vanilla and 1 cup pecans.

Nutrition Facts

1017.5 calories; protein 11.6g 23% DV; carbohydrates 120.3g 39% DV; fat 58.1g 89% DV; cholesterol 168.3mg 56% DV; sodium 409.1mg 16% DV.

SPICY ITALIAN SALAD

Prep: 30 mins Additional: 4 hrs - **Total:** 4 hrs 30 mins - **Servings:** 6

INGREDIENTS

- ½ cup canola oil
- ⅓ cup tarragon vinegar
- 1 tablespoon white sugar
- 1 teaspoon chopped fresh thyme
- ½ teaspoon dry mustard
- 2 cloves garlic, minced
- 1 (8 ounce) can artichoke hearts, drained and quartered
- 5 cups romaine lettuce - rinsed, dried, and chopped
- 1 red bell pepper, cut into strips
- 1 carrot, grated
- 1 red onion, thinly sliced
- ¼ cup black olives
- ¼ cup pitted green olives
- ½ cucumber, sliced
- 2 tablespoons grated Romano cheese
- ground black pepper to taste

DIRECTIONS

Step 1

In a medium container with a lid, mix canola oil, tarragon vinegar, sugar, thyme, dry mustard, and garlic. Cover, and shake until well blended. Place artichoke hearts into the mixture, cover, and marinate in the refrigerator 4 hours, or overnight.

Step 2

In a large bowl, toss together lettuce, red bell pepper, carrot, red onion, black olives, green olives, cucumber, and Romano cheese. Season with pepper. Pour in the artichoke and marinade mixture, and toss to coat.

Nutrition Facts

248.1 calories; protein 3.6g 7% DV; carbohydrates 13.2g 4% DV; fat 21.1g 32% DV; cholesterol 2.6mg 1% DV; sodium 462.2mg 19% DV.

SWEET ITALIAN GREEN BEANS

Prep: 10 mins - **Cook:** 15 mins - **Total:** 25 mins - **Servings:** 6

INGREDIENTS

- 4 slices bacon
- 3 medium (4-1/8" long)s green onions, chopped
- 2 cloves garlic, chopped
- 2 (15 ounce) cans green beans, drained
- 1 (14.5 ounce) can Italian-style diced tomatoes
- 1 pinch dried basil
- 1 pinch dried oregano
- ¼ cup brown sugar

DIRECTIONS

Step 1

Cook bacon in a skillet over medium heat until crisp. Remove from the pan to drain on paper towels. Reserve the grease in the skillet and add the onions; Cook and stir over medium heat until softened. Add garlic and Cook for about 30 seconds more. Remove from the heat.

Step 2

In a saucepan, combine the green beans, tomatoes, basil, oregano and brown sugar. Crumble in the bacon and add the onion and garlic from the skillet. Warm over medium heat until heated through, 5 to 10 minutes.

Nutrition Facts

159.3 calories; protein 4g 8% DV; carbohydrates 16.3g 5% DV; fat 8.5g 13% DV; cholesterol 12.7mg 4% DV; sodium 494.6mg 20% DV.

ITALIAN PASTA VEGGIE SALAD

Prep: 10 mins - **Cook:** 15 mins - **Total:** 25 mins - **Servings:** 8

INGREDIENTS
- 10 ounces fusilli pasta
- 1 onion, chopped
- 1 green bell pepper, chopped
- 2 medium whole (2-3/5" dia) (blank)s tomatoes, chopped
- 1 cup chopped mushrooms
- ¾ cup fat free Italian-style dressing

DIRECTIONS

Step 1
In a large pot of salted boiling water, Cook pasta until al dente, rinse under cold water and drain.

Step 2
In a large bowl, combine the pasta, onion, bell pepper, tomatoes and mushrooms. Pour enough dressing over to coat; toss and refrigerate until chilled.

Nutrition Facts
181.1 calories; protein 5.4g 11% DV; carbohydrates 38.1g 12% DV; fat 0.7g 1% DV; cholesterolmg; sodium 238mg 10% DV.

ITALIAN SAUSAGE AND GNOCCHI SOUP

Prep: 10 mins - **Cook:** 25 mins - **Total:** 35 mins - **Servings:** 4

INGREDIENTS
- ½ pound bulk Italian sausage
- ¼ cup butter
- ½ cup chopped yellow onion
- 1 teaspoon minced garlic
- ¼ cup all-purpose flour
- 1 cup heavy cream
- 3 ½ cups Swanson Unsalted Chicken Broth
- ½ cup chopped spinach
- ½ cup canned diced tomatoes
- 1 (16 ounce) package potato gnocchi
- 1 pinch salt and pepper to taste
- ¼ cup grated Parmesan cheese (or more to taste), for garnish

DIRECTIONS

Step 1

Heat a skillet over medium-high heat. Cook ground sausage until browned, breaking it up into small pieces, about 7 minutes. Transfer sausage to a bowl. Drain fat from skillet; wipe out skillet with a paper towel.

Step 2

Melt butter in skillet over medium heat, Stir in onion and saute until translucent, 2 or 3 minutes. Add garlic and Cook for another minute. Whisk in flour until evenly mixed into butter, 1 minute. Slowly pour in cream and Swanson Unsalted Chicken Broth. Whisk mixture until it comes to a boil, then immediately reduce heat to low. Simmer until mixture thickens, whisking occasionally, about 10 minutes.

Step 3

Return sausage to the skillet; add spinach, tomatoes, and gnocchi. Cook over medium heat until gnocchi is heated through, 2 to 3 minutes. Add dash of salt and pepper to taste. Garnish with Parmesan cheese.

Cook's Note:

This is a fast comfort soup, since the sausage is already spicy the Swanson(R) Unsalted Chicken Broth goes very well, allowing for all the flavors to come through. Any other vegetables can be added to one's own tastes!

Allstars are loyal Allrecipes community members, selected to be brand ambassadors based on onsite participation, interest, and commitment. Allstars may be compensated for their participation in the Allrecipes Allstar program.

Nutrition Facts

682.5 calories; protein 16.8g 34% DV; carbohydrates 33.6g 11% DV; fat 53.6g 83% DV; cholesterol 160mg 53% DV; sodium 866.4mg 35% DV.

ITALIAN WEDDING COOKIES II

Prep: 20 mins - **Cook:** 45 mins **Additional:** 55 mins - **Total:** 2 hrs - **Servings:** 36

INGREDIENTS

- 8 ounces almond paste
- 1 ½ cups butter, softened
- 1 cup white sugar
- 4 large eggs eggs
- 1 teaspoon almond extract
- 2 cups all-purpose flour
- ¼ teaspoon salt
- 5 drops green food coloring
- 5 drops yellow food coloring
- 5 drops red food coloring

- 1 (12 ounce) jar seedless raspberry jam, heated
- 1 (12 ounce) package semisweet chocolate chips, melted

DIRECTIONS

Step 1

Preheat oven to 350 degrees F (175 degrees C).

Step 2

Break almond paste into a large bowl, and beat in butter, sugar, eggs, and almond extract until light and fluffy. Beat in the flour and salt. Split batter into three equal portions, mixing one portion with green food coloring, one with yellow, and one with red. Spread each portion out to 1/4 inch thickness into the bottom of an ungreased 9x13 inch baking pan.

Step 3

Bake each layer for 12 to 15 minutes in the preheated oven, until lightly browned. Allow to cool.

Step 4

On a Cookie sheet or cutting board, stack the cakes, spreading tops of the first two layers with raspberry jam. Spread melted chocolate over top of the third layer. Chill in the refrigerator 1 hour, or until jam and chocolate are firm. Slice into small rectangles to serve.

Nutrition Facts

219.8 calories; protein 2.5g 5% DV; carbohydrates 25.9g 8% DV; fat 12.8g 20% DV; cholesterol 41mg 14% DV; sodium 80.1mg 3% DV.

NENNI'S ITALIAN PORK SAUSAGE

Prep: 2 hrs Additional: 8 hrs - **Total**: 10 hrs - **Servings**: 36

INGREDIENTS

- 9 pounds pork shoulder, cut into cubes
- 3 tablespoons garlic powder
- ¼ cup fennel seed
- 2 tablespoons crushed red pepper flakes
- 4 teaspoons salt
- 2 teaspoons ground black pepper
- 2 tablespoons dried parsley
- ½ cup dry white wine
- 15 feet 1 1/2 inch diameter hog casings, rinsed

DIRECTIONS

Step 1

Combine the pork cubes with the garlic powder, fennel seed, red pepper flakes, salt, black pepper, and parsley; grind through a coarse plate. Mix in the white wine and grind again. Stuff into the rinsed hog casings, twisting into 4-inch lengths. Cover and refrigerate overnight to allow the seasonings to infuse into the meat before Cooking or freezing.

Nutrition Facts

153.7 calories; protein 11.8g 24% DV; carbohydrates 1.2g; fat 10.8g 17% DV; cholesterol 44.7mg 15% DV; sodium 293.5mg 12% DV.

ITALIAN BBQ PORK CHOPS

Prep: 10 mins - **Cook:** 20 mins **Additional:** 10 mins - **Total:** 40 mins - **Servings:** 4

INGREDIENTS

- ¾ cup balsamic vinegar
- ½ cup ketchup
- ¼ cup brown sugar
- 1 clove garlic, minced
- 1 tablespoon Worcestershire sauce
- 1 tablespoon Dijon mustard
- ½ teaspoon salt
- ½ teaspoon freshly ground black pepper
- 4 (6 ounce) pork loin chops
- 1 pinch salt and freshly ground black pepper to taste

DIRECTIONS

Step 1

Stir the balsamic vinegar, ketchup, brown sugar, garlic, Worcestershire sauce, Dijon mustard, 1/2 teaspoon salt, and 1/2 teaspoon black pepper together in a saucepan over medium-low heat; cook the sauce at a simmer for 20 minutes. Remove from heat and allow to sit for 5 minutes.

Step 2

Preheat an outdoor grill for medium heat and lightly oil the grate.

Step 3

Season both sides of the pork chops with salt and black pepper. Brush the chops with the sauce from the saucepan.

Step 4

Cook the pork chops on the preheated grill until the pork is no longer pink in the center, about 5 minutes per side. An instant-read thermometer inserted into the center should read 145 degrees F (63 degrees C). Remove from the grill and allow to rest for 3 minutes before serving with the remaining sauce on the side.

Nutrition Facts

269.8 calories; protein 22.4g 45% DV; carbohydrates 30g 10% DV; fat 6.6g 10% DV; cholesterol 54.3mg 18% DV; sodium 807.1mg 32% DV.

HOMEMADE ITALIAN RED SAUCE

Prep: 10 mins - **Cook:** 2 hrs 10 mins - **Total:** 2 hrs 20 mins - **Servings:** 12

INGREDIENTS

- ½ cup olive oil
- 1 large onion, minced
- 3 cloves garlic, minced
- 4 cups water
- 2 (32 ounce) cans crushed diced tomatoes
- 1 (16 ounce) can tomato paste
- ¼ cup chopped fresh basil
- 1 teaspoon baking soda
- 1 teaspoon white sugar
- 1 pinch salt and ground black pepper to taste

DIRECTIONS

Step 1

Heat olive oil in a large saucepan over medium-high heat. Saute onion and garlic in hot oil until onion is translucent, 5 to 7 minutes.

Step 2

Reduce heat to medium-low. Add water, crushed tomatoes, tomato paste, basil, baking soda, and sugar; season with salt and pepper. Stir mixture, bring to a simmer, and cook until the sauce is thickened, about 2 hours.

Nutrition Facts

149.4 calories; protein 3.1g 6% DV; carbohydrates 13.9g 5% DV; fat 9.2g 14% DV; cholesterolmg; sodium 643.9mg 26% DV.

ITALIAN RICE PIE I

Servings: 8

INGREDIENTS

- 9 large eggs eggs
- 1 ½ cups white sugar
- 2 pounds ricotta cheese
- 1 teaspoon vanilla extract
- 2 cups heavy whipping cream
- 1 cup cooked white rice

- 1 (15 ounce) can crushed pineapple, drained

DIRECTIONS

Step 1

Beat eggs in very large bowl. Add sugar, mixing well. Stir in cheese and vanilla until smooth and creamy. Add heavy cream and stir. Fold in cooked rice and crushed pineapple.

Step 2

Pour into a 9 x 13 inch buttered pan.

Step 3

Bake at 325 degrees F (165 degrees C) for one hour. Check by inserting clean knife into center. If the pie is done, knife will come out clean. Top should be golden brown. Refrigerate until thoroughly cooled.

Nutrition Facts

646.2 calories; protein 22g 44% DV; carbohydrates 59.3g 19% DV; fat 36.7g 56% DV; cholesterol 326mg 109% DV; sodium 244mg 10% DV.

RICOTTA PIE (OLD ITALIAN RECIPE)

Prep: 45 mins - **Cook:** 45 mins **Additional:** 1 hr 30 mins - **Total:** 3 hrs - **Servings:** 24

INGREDIENTS

Pie Filling:

12 large eggs eggs

2 cups white sugar

2 teaspoons vanilla extract

3 pounds ricotta cheese

¼ cup miniature semisweet chocolate chips, or to taste

Sweet Crust:

- 4 cups all-purpose flour
- 5 teaspoons baking powder
- 1 cup white sugar
- ½ cup shortening, chilled
- 1 tablespoon shortening, chilled
- 4 large eggs eggs, lightly beaten
- 1 teaspoon vanilla extract
- 1 tablespoon milk

DIRECTIONS

Step 1

Beat the 12 eggs, 2 cups sugar and vanilla extract together in a large bowl. Stir in the ricotta cheese and the chocolate chips, if using (see Cook's Note). Set aside.

Step 2

Combine the flour, baking powder, and 1 cup sugar together. Cut in 1/2 cup plus 1 tablespoon shortening until the mixture resembles coarse crumbs. Mix in 4 beaten eggs and 1 teaspoon vanilla extract. Divide dough into 4 balls, wrap in plastic, and chill for at least 30 minutes.

Step 3

Preheat oven to 325 degrees F (165 degrees C). Grease two deep-dish pie plates.

Step 4

Roll out 2 of the balls to fit into the pie pans. Do not make the crust too thick, as it will expand during cooking. Do not flute the edges of the dough. Roll out the other 2 balls of dough and cut each into 8 narrow strips for the top of the crust. (Alternately, you can use cookie cutters and place the cutouts on the top of the pies.)

Step 5

Pour the ricotta filling evenly into the pie crusts. Top each pie with 8 narrow strips of dough or cookie cutouts. Brush top of pie with milk for shine, if desired. Place foil on the edge of crust.

Step 6

Bake in preheated oven for 20 to 30 minutes; remove foil. Rotate pies on the rack so they will bake evenly. Continue to bake until a knife inserted in the center of each pie comes out clean, 25 to 30 minutes more. Cool completely on wire racks. Refrigerate until serving.

Cook's Note:

Instead of the chocolate chips, you can use 1 tablespoon fresh lemon zest.

Nutrition Facts

352.1 calories; protein 12.9g 26% DV; carbohydrates 45.6g 15% DV; fat 13.4g 21% DV; cholesterol 141.6mg 47% DV; sodium 220.1mg 9% DV.

ITALIAN RICE PIE II

Prep: 50 mins - **Cook:** 1 hr 30 mins - **Total:** 2 hrs 20 mins - **Servings:** 16

INGREDIENTS

Crust

- 2 ½ cups all-purpose flour
- 1 tablespoon baking powder
- ¼ cup butter
- ½ cup white sugar
- 3 large eggs eggs
- ½ teaspoon vanilla extract

Filling

- 1 cup water

- ½ cup uncooked white rice
- 1 quart milk
- 1 (15 ounce) container ricotta cheese
- 1 ½ cups white sugar
- 1 tablespoon lemon juice
- 1 tablespoon grated lemon zest
- 6 large eggs eggs

DIRECTIONS

Step 1

Stir the flour and baking powder together in a bowl; set aside. In a second large bowl, cream the butter and 1/2 cup sugar until light and fluffy. Beat in 3 eggs, one at a time, and stir in the vanilla. Gradually beat in the flour mixture to make a soft dough. Divide the dough in half and shape into two balls. Working on a lightly floured surface, roll out each ball to fit two 10 inch pie plates. Line the pie plates with the crust, and refrigerate until needed.

Step 2

Bring the water to a boil in a saucepan, and stir in the rice. Reduce the heat to medium-low, cover, and cook for 20 minutes. Stir in the milk. Continue cooking, stirring frequently, until the mixture thickens. Set aside to cool.

Step 3

Preheat oven to 325 degrees F (165 degrees C).

Step 4

Meanwhile, beat the ricotta cheese, 1 1/2 cups sugar, lemon juice, lemon zest, and 6 eggs together in a mixing bowl until smooth and frothy. Stir in the cooled rice mixture until evenly blended. Pour into the pie shells.

Step 5

Bake pies in preheated oven until the filling is set and tops are golden brown, about 90 minutes. Cool on racks.

Nutrition Facts

323 calories; protein 11.1g 22% DV; carbohydrates 49.3g 16% DV; fat 9.2g 14% DV; cholesterol 125.4mg 42% DV; sodium 181.8mg 7% DV.

EASTER GRAIN PIE

Prep: 45 mins - **Cook:** 45 mins **Additional:** 1 day - **Total:** 1 day - **Servings:** 16

INGREDIENTS

- 5 cups water
- ½ cup whole wheat berries

- 6 large eggs eggs
- 1 cup white sugar
- 1 (8 ounce) package mixed candied fruit
- 1 ½ pounds ricotta cheese
- 1 teaspoon vanilla extract
- ½ teaspoon ground cinnamon
- 1 teaspoon grated lemon zest
- 2 teaspoons grated orange zest
- 1 tablespoon shortening
- 1 teaspoon salt
- 2 double (blank)s pastries for 9-inch lattice-top pies
- 2 tablespoons confectioners' sugar for dusting

DIRECTIONS

Step 1

Bring water to a boil in a large saucepan. Pour in wheat and allow to boil 40 minutes. As wheat is cooking, beat eggs in a large bowl while gradually adding 1 cup sugar to eggs. Mix in fruit, ricotta, vanilla extract, cinnamon, lemon rind, and orange rind.

Step 2

When wheat is ready, drain in a colander and rinse with warm water. Place 3/4 cup of cooked wheat in a small bowl, and mix in shortening and salt. Stir until shortening is melted, then stir wheat mixture into ricotta mixture along with the rest of the cooked wheat berries.

Step 3

Preheat oven to 375 degrees F (190 degrees C).

Step 4

Line two 9 inch pie pans with pastry. Cut remaining pastry into strips for tops of pies. Spoon half of filling into each pan. Cover with pastry strips to form lattice tops. Crimp edges.

Step 5

Bake in preheated oven for 45 minutes, until crust is golden brown. Sprinkle each pie with 1 tablespoon sugar and allow to cool at room temperature. Chill overnight before serving. Store any leftovers in refrigerator.

Nutrition Facts

454.2 calories; protein 10.6g 21% DV; carbohydrates 51.7g 17% DV; fat 23.3g 36% DV; cholesterol 91.9mg 31% DV; sodium 441.4mg 18% DV.

BEST ITALIAN SAUSAGE SOUP

Prep: 30 mins - **Cook:** 6 hrs - **Total:** 6 hrs 30 mins - **Servings:** 8

INGREDIENTS

- 1 ½ pounds sweet Italian sausage
- 2 cloves garlic, minced
- 2 small onions, chopped
- 2 (16 ounce) cans whole peeled tomatoes
- 1 ¼ cups dry red wine
- 5 cups beef broth
- ½ teaspoon dried basil
- ½ teaspoon dried oregano
- 2 medium (blank)s zucchini, sliced
- 1 green bell pepper, chopped
- 3 tablespoons chopped fresh parsley
- 1 (16 ounce) package spinach fettuccine pasta
- salt and pepper to taste

DIRECTIONS

Step 1

In a large pot, cook sausage over medium heat until brown. Remove with a slotted spoon, and drain on paper towels. Drain fat from pan, reserving 3 tablespoons.

Step 2

Cook garlic and onion in reserved fat for 2 to 3 minutes. Stir in tomatoes, wine, broth, basil, and oregano. Transfer to a slow cooker, and stir in sausage, zucchini, bell pepper, and parsley.

Step 3

Cover, and cook on Low for 4 to 6 hours.

Step 4

Bring a pot of lightly salted water to a boil. Cook pasta in boiling water until al dente, about 7 minutes. Drain water, and add pasta to the slow cooker. Simmer for a few minutes, and season with salt and pepper before serving.

Nutrition Facts

436.2 calories; protein 21g 42% DV; carbohydrates 43.5g 14% DV; fat 17.8g 27% DV; cholesterol 33.4mg 11% DV; sodium 1609.2mg 64% DV.

PIZZELLE-ITALIAN TRADITION

Servings: 6

INGREDIENTS

- 6 large eggs eggs

- 1 ½ cups white sugar
- 1 cup butter, melted
- 1 teaspoon lemon zest
- 1 teaspoon vanilla extract
- 3 ½ cups all-purpose flour
- 4 teaspoons baking powder

DIRECTIONS

Step 1

In a medium bowl, beat the eggs with an electric mixer until light. Add the sugar, butter, lemon zest and vanilla, mix well. Stir in the flour and baking powder.

Step 2

Heat pizzelle iron. Drop batter by teaspoonfuls onto the center of the patterns, close the lid and cook for about 30 seconds. Test the cooking time on the first one, because temperatures may vary. Remove cookies carefully from the iron and cool on wire racks.

Nutrition Facts

805.5 calories; protein 14.1g 28% DV; carbohydrates 107g 35% DV; fat 36.4g 56% DV; cholesterol 267.3mg 89% DV; sodium 614.5mg 25% DV.

CREAMY ITALIAN CHICKEN

Prep: 10 mins - **Cook:** 4 hrs - **Total:** 4 hrs 10 mins - **Servings:** 4

INGREDIENTS

- 3 breast half, bone and skin removed (blank)s skinless, boneless chicken breast halves, cubed
- ¼ cup water
- 1 packet dry Italian salad dressing mix (such as Kraft® Zesty Italian)
- 1 (10.75 ounce) can condensed cream of mushroom soup
- 1 (8 ounce) package cream cheese
- 1 (4.5 ounce) can mushroom pieces and stems, drained

DIRECTIONS

Step 1

Place the chicken breast pieces into the bottom of a slow cooker. Pour in water, and stir in the salad dressing mix. Cover the cooker, set on low, and cook 3 or more hours (see note).

Step 2

With an electric mixer, beat the soup, cream cheese, and mushrooms in a bowl until thoroughly combined. Mix with the chicken and any juices in the slow cooker. Cover and cook 1 more hour.

Cook's Notes

You can cook it slow all day with the first step as long as you add enough water and keep the chicken breasts whole until ready to do the next steps.

I add more or less water based on using fresh mushrooms or not. I like it creamy but not too runny or too thick.

Nutrition Facts

375.3 calories; protein 23.2g 46% DV; carbohydrates 11.8g 4% DV; fat 25.9g 40% DV; cholesterol 107.2mg 36% DV; sodium 1965.2mg 79% DV.

THE ITALIAN IRISHMAN'S PIE

Prep: 25 mins - **Cook:** 45 mins - **Total:** 1 hr 10 mins - **Servings:** 6

INGREDIENTS

- 1 tablespoon olive oil
- 1 pound bulk Italian sausage
- 2 tablespoons sausage drippings
- 2 tablespoons margarine
- 2 eaches apples, cored and sliced
- 1 large onion, sliced
- 1 pinch salt and ground black pepper to taste
- 1 teaspoon dried oregano
- 1 tablespoon all-purpose flour
- 1 cup water
- 3 cups prepared mashed potatoes
- 1 tablespoon melted margarine

DIRECTIONS

Step 1

Preheat oven to 350 degrees F (175 degrees C).

Step 2

Grease a 2-quart casserole dish.

Step 3

Heat olive oil in a skillet over medium heat; cook and stir Italian sausage until browned and crumbly, about 10 minutes. Use a slotted spoon to transfer sausage to prepared casserole dish. Drain drippings and reserve 2 tablespoons drippings in the skillet.

Step 4

Melt 2 tablespoons margarine in a separate skillet over medium heat; cook and stir apple and onion slices until tender, about 8 minutes. Place apple and onion in casserole dish with sausage.

Step 5

Lightly stir sausage, apple, and onion together; season with salt, black pepper, and oregano.

Step 6

Brown flour in reserved drippings in skillet over medium heat. Whisk water into flour until thick gravy forms, about 3 minutes.

Step 7

Pour gravy over sausage mixture in the casserole dish; spread mashed potatoes over the top with a spoon, creating peaks. Lightly brush mashed potatoes with 1 tablespoon melted margarine.

Step 8

Bake in the preheated oven until the potatoes are lightly browned and the sausage mixture is bubbling, about 30 minutes.

Nutrition Facts

373.2 calories; protein 12.6g 25% DV; carbohydrates 30.5g 10% DV; fat 22.5g 35% DV; cholesterol 31.8mg 11% DV; sodium 1011.6mg 41% DV.

ITALIAN TURKEY MEATBALLS

Servings: 8

INGREDIENTS

- 1 ½ pounds ground lean turkey
- ¼ cup shredded Parmesan cheese
- ⅔ cup dry Italian bread crumbs
- ⅓ cup chopped fresh parsley
- 3 tablespoons chopped fresh oregano
- 2 teaspoons chopped fresh rosemary
- 1 teaspoon dry mustard
- ¼ cup tomato sauce
- ¼ teaspoon salt
- ½ teaspoon crushed red pepper
- 3 eaches garlic cloves, minced
- 2 teaspoons Melt Organic Buttery Spread, softened

DIRECTIONS

Step 1

Preheat the oven to 400 degrees.

Step 2

Combine all the ingredients together except for the Melt; stir well in a bowl. Form around 30 balls out of the mixture. Put them on a broiler pan coated with the melted Melt. Bake around 15 minutes or until a cut meatball shows no pink inside. Serve with pasta and sauce or place on a sandwich.

Nutrition Facts

187.8 calories; protein 19.6g 39% DV; carbohydrates 8.1g 3% DV; fat 8.6g 13% DV; cholesterol 65.1mg 22% DV; sodium 351.3mg 14% DV.

ITALIAN CREAM CAKE

Servings: 12

INGREDIENTS

- 1 cup butter
- 5 large egg yolks egg yolks
- 1 teaspoon baking soda
- 2 cups all-purpose flour
- 5 large egg whites egg whites
- 2 cups white sugar
- 1 ½ cups buttermilk
- 1 cup chopped walnuts
- 1 cup flaked coconut
- 1 (8 ounce) package cream cheese
- ½ cup butter
- 3 ½ cups confectioners' sugar
- 1 teaspoon vanilla extract
- ¼ cup chopped walnuts

DIRECTIONS

Step 1

Cream together 1 cup butter or margarine, egg yolks, and 2 cups white sugar. Alternately mix in flour and buttermilk. Add baking soda. Mix in 1 cup walnuts and coconut.

Step 2

Beat egg whites, and fold into batter. Pour batter into three greased and floured 9 inch round cake pans.

Step 3

Bake for 20 to 25 minutes in a preheated 350 degrees F (175 degrees C) oven.

Step 4

Combine cream cheese, 1/2 cup butter or margarine, confectioners' sugar, and vanilla extract. Spread onto cooled cake. Top iced cake with chopped walnuts.

Nutrition Facts

759.3 calories; protein 9.5g 19% DV; carbohydrates 91.3g 30% DV; fat 41.5g 64% DV; cholesterol 168.1mg 56% DV; sodium 400.8mg 16% DV.

ITALIAN STYLE TURKEY MEATLOAF

Prep: 10 mins - **Cook:** 50 mins Additional: 5 mins - **Total:** 1 hr 5 mins - **Servings:** 6

INGREDIENTS

- 1 serving Cooking spray
- 1 pound ground turkey
- 1 egg
- ¼ cup Italian seasoned bread crumbs
- 1 teaspoon Italian seasoning
- ½ clove garlic, minced
- ½ teaspoon ground black pepper, or to taste
- ¼ teaspoon salt, or to taste
- 2 cups tomato sauce, divided

DIRECTIONS

Step 1

Preheat oven to 400 degrees F (200 degrees C). Prepare a baking dish with Cooking spray.

Step 2

Mix turkey, egg, bread crumbs, Italian seasoning, garlic, black pepper, and salt in a large bowl; shape into a loaf and put into prepared baking dish.

Step 3

Bake in preheated oven for 40 minutes. Spoon about half the tomato sauce over the loaf and continue baking until the meatloaf is no longer pink in the center, 10 to 15 minutes more. An instant-read thermometer inserted into the center should read at least 160 degrees F (70 degrees C). Rest meatloaf 5 to 10 minutes before slicing to serve.

Step 4

While the meatloaf rests, warm remaining tomato sauce in a small saucepan over medium-low heat; serve with the sliced meatloaf.

Nutrition Facts

162.8 calories; protein 17.8g 36% DV; carbohydrates 8.1g 3% DV; fat 7g 11% DV; cholesterol 86.8mg 29% DV; sodium 651mg 26% DV.

ITALIAN SEASONING

Prep: 5 mins - **Total:** 5 mins - **Servings:** 10

INGREDIENTS

- 2 tablespoons dried basil

- 2 tablespoons dried oregano
- 2 tablespoons dried thyme
- 2 tablespoons dried marjoram
- 1 tablespoon dried rosemary
- 1 tablespoon dried sage

DIRECTIONS

Step 1

In a food processor, combine basil, oregano, thyme, marjoram, rosemary and sage. Blend for 1 minute, or until desired consistency is achieved.

Nutrition Facts

9.5 calories; protein 0.4g 1% DV; carbohydrates 1.9g 1% DV; fat 0.3g; cholesterolmg; sodium 1.3mg.

ITALIAN STYLE SAUSAGE

Prep: 10 mins - **Cook:** 15 mins - **Total:** 25 mins - **Servings:** 6

INGREDIENTS

- 1 teaspoon ground black pepper
- 1 teaspoon dried parsley
- 1 teaspoon Italian-style seasoning
- ½ teaspoon garlic powder
- ⅛ teaspoon crushed red pepper flakes
- ¾ teaspoon crushed anise seeds
- ½ teaspoon paprika
- ½ teaspoon dried minced onion
- 2 teaspoons salt
- 2 pounds ground pork

DIRECTIONS

Step 1

In a small bowl, combine the ground black pepper, parsley, Italian-style seasoning, garlic powder, crushed red pepper flakes, anise, paprika, minced onion flakes and salt; mix well.

Step 2

Place pork in a separate large bowl and add the spice mix to it. Mix this thoroughly with your hands.

Step 3

In a large skillet over medium high heat, saute the seasoned pork for 10 minutes, or until well browned and crumbly.

Nutrition Facts

314.5 calories; protein 27g 54% DV; carbohydrates 0.9g; fat 21.8g 34% DV; cholesterol 98.1mg 33% DV; sodium 852.1mg 34% DV.

ITALIAN SAUSAGE AND ZUCCHINI

Prep: 20 mins - **Cook:** 25 mins - **Total:** 45 mins - **Servings:** 6

INGREDIENTS

- 1 ½ pounds Italian sausage links
- 2 small zucchini, sliced
- 1 small yellow squash, sliced
- ½ cup chopped onion
- 1 (14.5 ounce) can stewed tomatoes, with liquid

DIRECTIONS

Step 1

In a large skillet over medium heat, brown the Italian sausage until the inside is no longer pink. Cut sausage into 1/4 inch slices, and continue Cooking until browned.

Step 2

Stir in the zucchini, yellow squash, and onion; Cook and stir for 2 minutes. Pour in the tomatoes, with liquid. Reduce heat, cover, and simmer for 10 to 15 minutes.

Nutrition Facts

300.9 calories; protein 16.5g 33% DV; carbohydrates 10.5g 3% DV; fat 21.6g 33% DV; cholesterol 44.6mg 15% DV; sodium 1096.8mg 44% DV.

ITALIAN CHICKEN MARINADE

Prep: 15 mins - **Cook:** 15 mins Additional: 4 hrs - **Total:** 4 hrs 30 mins - **Servings:** 4

INGREDIENTS

- 1 (16 ounce) bottle Italian-style salad dressing
- 1 teaspoon garlic powder
- 1 teaspoon salt
- 4 breast half, bone and skin removed (blank)s skinless, boneless chicken breast halves

DIRECTIONS

Step 1

In a shallow baking dish, mix the salad dressing, garlic powder, and salt. Place the chicken in the bowl, and turn to coat. Marinate in the refrigerator at least 4 hours. (For best results, marinate overnight.)

Step 2

Preheat the grill for high heat.

Step 3

Lightly oil grate. Discard marinade, and grill chicken 8 minutes on each side, or until juices run clear.

Note

The nutrition data for this recipe includes information for the full amount of the marinade ingredients. Depending on marinating time, ingredients, Cook time, etc., the actual amount of the marinade consumed will vary.

Nutrition Facts

454.6 calories; protein 25.1g 50% DV; carbohydrates 12g 4% DV; fat 34.2g 53% DV; cholesterol 67.2mg 22% DV; sodium 2469.2mg 99% DV.

PARTY ITALIAN WEDDING SOUP

Prep: 15 mins - **Cook:** 1 hr - **Total:** 1 hr 15 mins - **Servings:** 12

INGREDIENTS

- 1 (48 fluid ounce) can chicken broth
- 1 (10 ounce) package frozen chopped spinach, thawed and drained
- 2 medium (2-1/2" dia)s onions, chopped
- 2 cups chopped carrot
- 2 stalks celery, chopped
- 1 pound ground beef
- 1 cup dry bread crumbs
- 1 egg
- 1 pound skinless, boneless chicken breast halves - cut into chunks
- 3 ounces dry pasta
- salt and pepper to taste

DIRECTIONS

Step 1

In a large pot over medium heat, combine the chicken broth, spinach, onions, carrots and celery. Mix well and allow to simmer.

Step 2

In a separate large bowl, combine the ground beef, bread crumbs and egg and mix well. Form mixture into 1/2 inch diameter meatballs and carefully drop them into the soup.

Step 3

Put chunks of chicken breast into the soup and reduce heat to low. Allow the soup to simmer for 1 hour. Add the pasta 30 minutes before serving and season with salt and pepper to taste.

Nutrition Facts

260.3 calories; protein 19.7g 39% DV; carbohydrates 17g 6% DV; fat 12.2g 19% DV; cholesterol 81mg

27% DV; sodium 732.5mg 29% DV.

ITALIAN LEMON CREAM CAKE

Prep: 20 mins - **Cook**: 30 mins **Additional**:4 hrs - **Total**: 4 hrs 50 mins - **Servings**: 12

INGREDIENTS

- 1 serving Cooking spray
- Cake:
- 1 (16.25 ounce) package white cake mix
- ¾ cup milk
- 1 tablespoon milk
- 2 large eggs eggs
- 3 ½ tablespoons vegetable oil
- Crumb Topping:
- 2 tablespoons butter, melted
- ½ teaspoon vanilla extract

Filling:

- 4 ounces cream cheese, softened
- ⅔ cup confectioners' sugar, divided, plus more for dusting
- 3 tablespoons lemon juice
- 1 teaspoon grated lemon zest
- 2 cups heavy whipping cream

DIRECTIONS

Step 1

Preheat oven to 350 degrees F (175 degrees C). Spray the bottom of a 10-inch springform pan with Cooking spray.

Step 2

Measure 1 cup cake mix; set aside for crumb topping. Place the remaining cake mix in a large bowl; add 3/4 cup plus 1 tablespoon milk, eggs, and oil. Beat cake mix mixture using an electric mixer until batter is thoroughly combined, about 2 minutes. Pour batter into the prepared pan.

Step 3

Mix melted butter and vanilla extract together in a bowl; stir in reserved 1 cup cake mix until mixture is crumbly. Sprinkle crumbs over top of cake batter.

Step 4

Bake in the preheated oven until a toothpick inserted in the center of the cake comes out clean, 30 to 35 minutes. Cool cake to room temperature in the pan.

Step 5

Beat cream cheese, 1/3 cup confectioners' sugar, lemon juice, and lemon zest together in a bowl until smooth and creamy. Beat cream and remaining 1/3 cup confectioners' sugar together in a separate bowl using an electric mixer until stiff peaks form. Fold cream cheese mixture into whipped cream.

Step 6

Remove cake from springform pan. Cut cake horizontally into 2 layers using a serrated knife; remove top layer. Spread filling onto the bottom cake layer; place top cake over filling. Refrigerate cake for at least 4 hours. Dust cake with more confectioners' sugar before serving.

Nutrition Facts

434.5 calories; protein 4.9g 10% DV; carbohydrates 39.5g 13% DV; fat 29.2g 45% DV; cholesterol 102.1mg 34% DV; sodium 330.2mg 13% DV.

ITALIAN BEEF SANDWICHES

Cook: 2 hrs - **Additional:** 1 day - **Total:** 1 day - **Servings:** 8

INGREDIENTS

- 4 pounds boneless rump roast
- 6 cloves garlic, slivered
- 1 cup water
- 1 tablespoon salt
- 1 tablespoon coarsely ground black pepper
- 1 tablespoon crushed red pepper
- 1 tablespoon dried oregano

DIRECTIONS

Step 1

Preheat oven to 250 degrees F (120 degrees C). Make slits in roast with a sharp knife, and insert garlic slivers. Place roast in a pan not much larger than the roast. Pour water into pan, and season roast with salt, black pepper, red pepper, and oregano.

Step 2

Cover, and bake in preheated oven for 2 hours, basting occasionally. Remove from oven, and let cool in roasting pan. Meat should be very rare. Wrap tightly and refrigerate overnight.

Step 3

The next day, Remove roast from pan, and slice as thinly as possible. Add a little water to roasting pan, and heat on stovetop, but do not boil. Stir to blend seasonings. When au jus is hot, add sliced beef just long enough to heat through. Serve on crusty Italian bread with au jus available for dipping.

Nutrition Facts

493.8 calories; protein 45.2g 90% DV; carbohydrates 2.3g 1% DV; fat 32.7g 50% DV; cholesterol 138.3mg

46% DV; sodium 985.2mg 39% DV.

SPICY ITALIAN PORK CUTLETS

Prep: 15 mins - **Cook:** 20 mins - **Total:** 35 mins - **Servings:** 4

INGREDIENTS

- ¼ cup extra virgin olive oil, divided
- 4 raw chop with refuse, 120 g; (blank) 4.225 ounces boneless pork chops, pounded to 1/4 inch thick
- 1 pinch salt and pepper to taste
- 4 cloves garlic, thinly sliced
- 1 large tomato, diced
- ⅓ cup chicken broth
- ¼ cup dry white wine
- 3 tablespoons minced fresh parsley
- ¼ teaspoon red pepper flakes

DIRECTIONS

Step 1

Heat 2 tablespoons olive oil in a skillet over medium-high heat. Season the pork chops with salt and pepper, and quickly sear on both sides. Remove from heat, and set aside.

Step 2

Heat the remaining olive oil in the skillet over medium-high heat, and saute the garlic about 30 seconds. Mix in the tomato, chicken broth, wine, parsley, and red pepper flakes. Cook and stir until thickened, about 2 minutes.

Step 3

Return the pork chops to the skillet, and continue Cooking 5 to 10 minutes, to an internal temperature of 145 degrees F (63 degrees C). Serve pork with the tomato and broth mixture from the skillet.

Nutrition Facts

260.4 calories; protein 16.1g 32% DV; carbohydrates 3.5g 1% DV; fat 18.7g 29% DV; cholesterol 38.7mg 13% DV; sodium 107.2mg 4% DV.

QUICK ITALIAN PASTA SALAD

Prep: 15 mins - **Cook:** 10 mins - **Total:** 25 mins - **Servings:** 12

INGREDIENTS

- 1 (12 ounce) package tri-color rotini pasta
- ¾ pound Italian salami, finely diced
- ½ green bell pepper, sliced

- ½ red bell pepper, sliced
- ½ red onion, chopped
- 1 cup Italian-style salad dressing
- 1 (6 ounce) can sliced black olives
- 8 ounces small fresh mozzarella balls (ciliegine)
- 3 (.7 ounce) packages dry Italian-style salad dressing mix, or to taste
- ½ cup shredded Parmesan cheese

DIRECTIONS

Step 1

Bring a large pot of lightly salted water to a boil; Cook rotini at a boil until tender yet firm to the bite, about 8 minutes; drain and rinse with cold water until cool.

Step 2

Combine pasta, salami, green bell pepper, red bell pepper, onion, salad dressing, olives, and mozzarella cheese in a large bowl. Mix dry salad dressing into pasta; sprinkle with Parmesan cheese.

Nutrition Facts

370.9 calories; protein 15.2g 30% DV; carbohydrates 29.2g 9% DV; fat 21g 32% DV; cholesterol 46mg 15% DV; sodium 1893.1mg 76% DV.

PASTA SAUCE WITH ITALIAN SAUSAGE

Prep: 30 mins - **Cook:** 1 hr - **Total:** 1 hr 30 mins - **Servings:** 6

INGREDIENTS

- 1 pound Italian sausage links
- ½ pound lean ground beef
- 1 tablespoon olive oil
- 1 onion, chopped
- 1 clove garlic, chopped
- 1 (16 ounce) can canned tomatoes
- 1 (15 ounce) can canned tomato sauce
- 1 teaspoon salt
- ¼ teaspoon ground black pepper
- 1 teaspoon dried basil
- 1 teaspoon dried oregano
- 1 bay leaf

DIRECTIONS

Step 1

Removed casing from sausage links and cut into 1/2 inch slices. In a large skillet, brown sausage over medium heat for about 10 minutes; remove and set aside.

Step 2

In a large skillet, heat ground beef, olive oil, garlic and onion over medium heat until meat is nicely browned; drain.

Step 3

Pour in tomatoes and tomato sauce; mix in salt, ground black pepper, basil, oregano, bay leaf and Cooked sausage. Simmer uncovered for 1 hour, stirring occasionally.

Step 4

Bring a large pot of lightly salted water to a boil. Add pasta and Cook for 8 to 10 minutes or until al dente; drain.

Step 5

Mix Cooked sauce with hot pasta and remove bay leaf from sauce before serving.

Nutrition Facts

339.2 calories; protein 18.5g 37% DV; carbohydrates 11.4g 4% DV; fat 24.6g 38% DV; cholesterol 58.1mg 19% DV; sodium 1517.8mg 61% DV.

THREE ANIMAL ITALIAN MEATBALLS

Prep: 30 mins **- Cook:** 30 mins **- Total:** 1 hr **- Servings:** 8

INGREDIENTS

- 1 pound ground beef
- 1 pound ground turkey
- 1 pound ground Italian sausage
- 1 large onion, diced
- 2 large eggs eggs
- ½ cup Italian-style seasoned bread crumbs
- ½ cup quick Cooking oats
- 2 tablespoons Italian-style seasoning
- 1 cup vegetable oil, or as needed

DIRECTIONS

Step 1

Preheat oven to 350 degrees F (175 degrees C).

Step 2

Combine ground meat, onion, eggs, bread crumbs, oats, and seasoning in a large bowl. Shape into 2-inch diameter balls.

Step 3

Heat enough vegetable oil in a large saute pan to be 1/2 inch deep. Brown meatballs in hot oil for about 5 minutes. Transfer to a glass baking dish.

Step 4

Bake in preheated oven for 25 minutes.

Tips

We have determined the nutritional value of oil for frying based on a retention value of 10% after Cooking. The exact amount will vary depending on Cooking time and temperature, ingredient density, and the specific type of oil used.

Nutrition Facts

635.4 calories; protein 31.8g 64% DV; carbohydrates 12.8g 4% DV; fat 50.9g 78% DV; cholesterol 145mg 48% DV; sodium 662.9mg 27% DV.

JENNI'S ITALIAN FARRO PILAF

Prep: 15 mins - **Cook:** 40 mins - **Total:** 55 mins - **Servings:** 6

INGREDIENTS

- 1 cup semi-pearled farro, rinsed
- 2 teaspoons chicken bouillon
- 2 cups water
- ⅔ cup sun-dried tomatoes packed in olive oil with garlic, drained and chopped
- 1 (8 ounce) package fresh mushrooms, cubed
- 1 tablespoon dried basil
- 1 pound yellow squash, cubed
- ¼ cup grated Parmesan cheese

DIRECTIONS

Instructions Checklist

Step 1

Bring farro, chicken bouillon, and water to a boil in a saucepan. Reduce heat to medium-low, cover, and simmer until farro is tender and the liquid has been absorbed, 20 to 25 minutes. Drain any excess water.

Step 2

Cook and stir sun-dried tomatoes and mushrooms with basil in a skillet over medium heat until mushrooms are slightly softened, about 5 minutes. Add squash and cook until tender, about 10 more minutes. Cook and stir farro with squash mixture until heated through, 2 to 3 minutes. Sprinkle farro pilaf with Parmesan cheese.

Nutrition Facts

161.5 calories; protein 7.5g 15% DV; carbohydrates 29.6g 10% DV; fat 3.8g 6% DV; cholesterol 2.9mg 1% DV; sodium 101.1mg 4% DV.

FUZZY ITALIAN NAVEL

Prep: 1 min - **Total:** 1 min - **Servings:** 1

INGREDIENTS

- 1 (1.5 fluid ounce) jigger grenadine syrup
- 2 (1.5 fluid ounce) jiggers peach schnapps
- 1 cup orange juice
- 2 fluid ounces carbonated water

DIRECTIONS

Step 1

Measure grenadine and peach schnapps into a glass of ice. Fill with orange juice to within 1 inch of the glass rim; top with carbonated water.

Nutrition Facts

581.1 calories; protein 1.8g 4% DV; carbohydrates 103.4g 34% DV; fat 0.8g 1% DV; cholesterolmg; sodium 25.4mg 1% DV.

SAVORY ITALIAN SAUSAGE SAUCE

Prep: 20 mins - **Cook:** 1 hr 15 mins - **Total:** 1 hr 35 mins - **Servings:** 4

INGREDIENTS

- 2 tablespoons olive oil
- 4 cloves garlic, minced
- 1 pound Italian sausage
- 4 medium (4-1/8" long)s green onions, chopped
- 1 (8 ounce) package fresh mushrooms, sliced
- 1 tablespoon dried basil
- 1 tablespoon dried oregano
- 1 (15 ounce) can tomato sauce
- 1 (14.5 ounce) can stewed tomatoes
- 1 (6 ounce) can tomato paste
- ½ cup water
- ½ cup red wine
- 1 teaspoon red pepper flakes
- 2 tablespoons white sugar
- 1 pinch salt and pepper to taste

DIRECTIONS

Step 1

Heat olive oil in a large skillet over medium-high heat. Saute garlic until browned. Add sausage and cook for 4 minutes, breaking apart with a spoon. Add green onions and cook until sausage is evenly browned, about 10 minutes.

Step 2

Stir in mushrooms, basil and oregano; cook for 5 minutes. Stir in tomato sauce, stewed tomatoes, and tomato paste. Add water, red wine, red pepper flakes, and sugar. Season with salt and pepper to taste. Reduce heat to low and simmer for at least 1 hour.

Nutrition Facts

495.2 calories; protein 21g 42% DV; carbohydrates 36.3g 12% DV; fat 29.2g 45% DV; cholesterol 44.6mg 15% DV; sodium 2101.7mg 84% DV.

ITALIAN STYLE POT ROAST

Prep: 10 mins - **Cook:** 2 hrs 40 mins - **Total:** 2 hrs 50 mins - **Servings:** 8

INGREDIENTS

- 3 ½ pounds boneless chuck roast
- 2 tablespoons vegetable oil
- 1 (14.5 ounce) can stewed tomatoes
- 1 ½ cups pizza sauce
- ½ cup grated Parmesan cheese
- 4 teaspoons Worcestershire sauce
- 2 cloves garlic, minced
- 2 teaspoons salt
- 2 teaspoons dried oregano
- ½ teaspoon ground black pepper
- ½ pound fresh mushrooms, sliced
- 3 tablespoons cornstarch
- 3 tablespoons water
- 1 (12 ounce) package egg noodles

DIRECTIONS

Step 1

Heat a Dutch oven over medium-high heat, and brown meat on all sides in hot oil.

Step 2

In large bowl combine tomatoes, pizza sauce, cheese, Worcestershire sauce, garlic, salt, oregano, and pepper. Pour over meat. Cover and simmer over medium heat for 2 hours, turning meat each half hour.

Step 3

Remove meat from pan, and cool slightly. Skim fat from pan juices. Measure juices, and add enough water to make 6 cups liquid. Return liquid to Dutch oven. Blend cornstarch and 3 tablespoons cold water; stir into pan juices. Cook and stir till thickened and bubbly.

Step 4

Slice meat thinly against the grain. Return meat to pot, and add mushrooms. Simmer for 30 minutes longer.

Step 5

Cook pasta in a large pot of boiling water until done. Drain. To serve, place meat slices over hot noodles, and pour some sauce over. Pass remaining sauce.

Nutrition Facts

742.3 calories; protein 44.8g 90% DV; carbohydrates 42.5g 14% DV; fat 42.9g 66% DV; cholesterol 181.7mg 61% DV; sodium 1208mg 48% DV.

ITALIAN SAUSAGE STUFFED SHELLS

Servings: 8

INGREDIENTS

- 1 (16 ounce) package jumbo pasta shells
- 3 teaspoons vegetable oil, divided
- 1 pound bulk Italian sausage
- 1 (16 ounce) package finely shredded mozzarella cheese, divided
- 1 teaspoon dried Italian seasoning, plus more for garnish if desired
- 1 (24 ounce) jar prepared marinara sauce

DIRECTIONS

Step 1

Preheat oven to 350 degrees F (175 degrees C). Lightly oil a 9x13 baking dish.

Step 2

Bring a large pot of lightly salted water to a boil. Cook shells in the boiling water, stirring occasionally until tender yet firm to the bite, about 10 to 12 minutes. Drain. Lightly oil a rimmed baking sheet; place drained pasta on baking sheet to cool.

Step 3

Heat 2 teaspoons vegetable oil over medium-high heat in a heavy skillet. Cook and crumble sausage until it has lost its pink color and begins to brown. Remove from heat; drain off grease.

Step 4

Stir half of the shredded cheese and the Italian seasoning into the browned sausage. Spoon mixture into the pasta shells (1 to 2 tablespoons per shell). Arrange stuffed shells in prepared baking dish. Pour marinara sauce evenly over the shells. Top with remaining shredded cheese. Cover tightly with aluminum foil.

Step 5

Bake in preheated oven until heated through and bubbly, about 30 minutes. Remove foil; bake until browned, 5 to 10 more minutes. Sprinkle with a pinch of Italian seasoning, if desired.

Cook's Note:

If you don't like a lot of sauce, adjust to suit your personal tastes. And if you prefer, you can sprinkle parsley flakes on the baked shells instead of Italian seasoning.

Nutrition Facts

578.2 calories; protein 30.2g 60% DV; carbohydrates 57.3g 19% DV; fat 24.6g 38% DV; cholesterol 60.3mg 20% DV; sodium 1171.4mg 47% DV.

ITALIAN MEAT SAUCE I

Prep: 45 mins - **Cook:** 5 hrs - **Total:** 5 hrs 45 mins - **Servings:** 12

INGREDIENTS

- 4 tablespoons olive oil
- 1 onion, chopped
- 6 cloves garlic, sliced
- 3 (15 ounce) cans seasoned tomato sauce
- 3 (14.5 ounce) cans diced tomatoes with juice
- 6 cups water
- 8 (6 ounce) cans tomato paste
- 2 pounds sweet Italian sausage
- 2 pounds ground sirloin
- 4 tablespoons chopped fresh parsley, divided
- 1 cup grated Romano cheese
- 2 tablespoons dried oregano
- salt and pepper to taste
- 1 pound pork meat, cubed
- 1 cup dry bread crumbs
- 3 tablespoons garlic powder
- ⅓ cup grated Parmesan cheese
- 2 large eggs eggs

DIRECTIONS

Step 1

In large pot heat 2 tablespoons olive oil over low heat. Add chopped onion and two-thirds of sliced garlic. Saute 5 minutes. Add tomato sauce, diced tomatoes, water and tomato paste. Simmer.

Step 2

Meanwhile, in large skillet, heat remaining 2 tablespoons of olive oil over medium heat. Saute remaining garlic 1 to 2 minutes. Add sausage and brown, about three minutes on each side. After browning, cover and reduce heat. Cook for 10 minutes, remove from heat, and cut sausages into halves. Add to tomato mixture.

Step 3

Cook pork over medium heat in sausage skillet until brown. Add to tomato mixture. Add 3 tablespoons parsley, Romano, oregano, salt and pepper to tomato sauce. Continue to simmer over low heat.

Step 4

Preheat oven to 375 degrees F (190 degrees C). Cover a cookie sheet with aluminum foil. In large bowl combine ground sirloin, bread crumbs, garlic powder, remaining parsley, parmesan and eggs. Form 1 inch balls and place on cookie sheet. Cook until golden brown, about 20 minutes. Add meatballs to sauce. Continue to cook sauce for 5 hours. Serve over fusilli or ravioli.

Nutrition Facts

660.6 calories; protein 41.9g 84% DV; carbohydrates 46.4g 15% DV; fat 35.5g 55% DV; cholesterol 133.7mg 45% DV; sodium 2541.6mg 102% DV.

ITALIAN CABBAGE SALAD

Prep: 15 mins **Additional:** 1 hr - **Total:** 1 hr 15 mins - **Servings:** 4

INGREDIENTS

Dressing:

- 7 tablespoons canola oil
- 2 tablespoons tarragon vinegar
- 2 tablespoons lemon juice
- 1 teaspoon white sugar
- 1 teaspoon salt
- ½ teaspoon ground black pepper

Salad:

- ½ head green cabbage, thinly sliced
- ½ red onion, thinly sliced

DIRECTIONS

Step 1

Whisk oil, vinegar, lemon juice, sugar, salt, and pepper together until emulsified.

Step 2

Toss cabbage and red onion together in a salad bowl. Drizzle dressing over the salad; toss to coat.

Step 3

Refrigerate salad 1 hour before serving.

Nutrition Facts

261.5 calories; protein 2.1g 4% DV; carbohydrates 10.7g 3% DV; fat 24.7g 38% DV; cholesterolmg; sodium 608.7mg 24% DV.

ITALIAN SAUSAGE SPAGHETTI SQUASH

Prep: 20 mins - **Cook:** 1 hr 40 mins - **Total:** 2 hrs - **Servings:** 12

INGREDIENTS

- 1 (3 pound) spaghetti squash, halved and seeded
- 1 pound ground Italian sausage
- 1 small onion, chopped
- 1 rib celery, chopped
- 1 small carrot, chopped
- 1 (15 ounce) can diced tomatoes with basil, garlic, and oregano
- 1 ½ cups chicken broth
- ½ (6 ounce) can tomato paste
- 3 cloves garlic, pressed
- 1 cup shredded mozzarella cheese

DIRECTIONS

Step 1

Preheat oven to 400 degrees F (200 degrees C). Line a baking sheet with parchment paper. Place squash, cut sides down, on baking sheet.

Step 2

Bake squash in the preheated oven until it starts to soften, about 25 minutes. Reduce oven temperature to 350 degrees F (175 degrees C) and continue baking until easily pierced with a knife, about 25 minutes more. Remove from the oven and cool until easily handled.

Step 3

Cook sausage in a large skillet over medium heat until browned, about 5 minutes; remove from skillet. Add onion, celery, and carrot to the skillet; cook and stir in sausage drippings until starting to soften, about 5 minutes. Stir cooked sausage, diced tomatoes, chicken broth, tomato paste, and garlic into the skillet. Simmer sauce until flavors combine, about 15 minutes.

Step 4

Use a fork to scrape insides of squash into spaghetti strands. Transfer strands to a 9x13-inch casserole dish. Spoon sauce over strands and stir to combine. Cover with mozzarella cheese.

Step 5

Bake in the preheated oven oven until bubbly and golden brown, about 25 minutes.

Nutrition Facts

167.8 calories; protein 8.8g 18% DV; carbohydrates 13g 4% DV; fat 9.3g 14% DV; cholesterol 20.9mg 7% DV; sodium 510.2mg 20% DV.

CHUNKY ITALIAN SPAGHETTI SAUCE

Prep: 10 mins - **Cook:** 35 mins - **Total:** 45 mins - **Servings:** 6

INGREDIENTS

- 2 (16 ounce) cans diced tomatoes
- 2 (15 ounce) cans tomato sauce
- 1 tablespoon garlic powder
- 2 teaspoons white sugar
- 2 teaspoons dried parsley
- ½ teaspoon salt
- ¼ teaspoon dried oregano
- ¼ teaspoon dried basil
- ¼ teaspoon ground black pepper

DIRECTIONS

Step 1

Combine diced tomatoes, tomato sauce, garlic powder, sugar, parsley, salt, oregano, basil, and pepper in a saucepan; bring to a boil. Lower heat to medium-low, cover saucepan, and simmer until flavors blend, about 30 minutes.

Cook's Note:

This is delicious to simmer meatballs in - add cooked meatballs in during the last 15 minutes of simmering.

Nutrition Facts

75.8 calories; protein 3.4g 7% DV; carbohydrates 15.1g 5% DV; fat 0.3g; cholesterolmg; sodium 1166.3mg 47% DV.

TARRADLS (ITALIAN PEPPER RINGS)

Servings: 24

INGREDIENTS

- 2 cups warm water (110 degrees F/45 degrees C)
- 1 (.25 ounce) package active dry yeast
- 1 cup olive oil
- 1 tablespoon salt
- 7 cups all-purpose flour

- 1 teaspoon ground black pepper
- 1 cup almonds

DIRECTIONS

Step 1

In a large bowl dissolve the yeast in the warm water and let stand for 5 minutes.

Step 2

Add the olive oil and 4 cups of the flour to the yeast mixture. Stir with a wooden spoon until well incorporated and the pepper and a more flour a little at a time until the dough is able to be kneaded.

Step 3

Place dough on a floured board and add more flour. Make sure dough remains moist. It should be slightly more moist than normal bread dough. Knead dough for 5 minutes. Cover with a warm moist cloth and let rise in a warm place for about 3 hours.

Step 4

Place almonds and about 2 cups of water in a small saucepan and bring almost to a boil. Let sit for 10 minutes. Drain and peel then place the almonds on a baking sheet and bake in a preheated 350 degree oven for 10 minutes. Remove from oven and let cool.

Step 5

Once dough is ready, divide it into thirds and roll each third out to 1/4 inch thick squares. Cut into 1 inch wide strips. Place about 3 or 4 almond in a row on end of the strips and fold the other end over and seal the nuts well. Twist dough together to form rings and pinch ends together. They should be about 2 to 2 1/2 inch rings. Place the rings on a parchment lined baking sheet.

Step 6

Bake in a preheat 350 degrees F (175 degrees C) oven for 30 minutes or until nice and brown. To make them more crispy place them in a roasting pan and return to the oven as it cools.

Nutrition Facts

247.6 calories; protein 5.1g 10% DV; carbohydrates 29.2g 9% DV; fat 12.4g 19% DV; cholesterolmg; sodium 291.8mg 12% DV.

ITALIAN STYLE CHILI

Prep: 5 mins - **Cook:** 40 mins - **Total:** 45 mins - **Servings:** 6

INGREDIENTS

- 1 pound lean ground beef
- ¾ cup chopped onion
- 1 (26 ounce) jar three cheese spaghetti sauce
- 1 ½ cups water
- 2 teaspoons sugar

- 1 (14.5 ounce) can diced tomatoes
- 1 (4 ounce) can sliced mushrooms
- 2 ounces sliced pepperoni
- 1 tablespoon beef bouillon
- 1 tablespoon chili powder
- 1 (14.5 ounce) can kidney beans, drained and rinsed
- 1 cup shredded Cheddar cheese, for garnish

DIRECTIONS

Step 1

Crumble ground beef into a large stock pot over medium-high heat. Add onions, and cook, stirring, until beef is evenly browned. Drain grease, if necessary.

Step 2

Pour in the spaghetti sauce, water, sugar, tomatoes, mushrooms, pepperoni, bouillon, chili powder and kidney beans. Bring to a boil. Reduce heat, and simmer uncovered for 30 minutes, stirring occasionally, to blend flavors.

Nutrition Facts

488.9 calories; protein 28.3g 57% DV; carbohydrates 34.5g 11% DV; fat 26g 40% DV; cholesterol 82.1mg 27% DV; sodium 1407.4mg 56% DV.

ITALIAN AMARETTO MARGARITAS

Prep: 10 mins - **Total:** 10 mins - **Servings:** 4

INGREDIENTS

- 4 fluid ounces amaretto liqueur, plus additional
- 4 teaspoons white sugar
- 6 fluid ounces frozen limeade concentrate
- 6 fluid ounces tequila
- ½ cup orange juice
- 6 cups ice

DIRECTIONS

Step 1

Dip the rims of 4 margarita glasses in amaretto, then into sugar; set aside. Pour the limeaid, tequila, amaretto, orange juice, and ice into the bowl of a blender. Puree until smooth, then pour into prepared glasses.

Nutrition Facts

375.1 calories; protein 0.2g; carbohydrates 55.4g 18% DV; fat 0.2g; cholesterolmg; sodium 12.6mg 1% DV.

ITALIAN ONION CUCUMBER SALAD

Prep: 20 mins **Additional:** 1 hr - **Total:** 1 hr 20 mins - **Servings:** 4

INGREDIENTS

- 2 medium (blank)s cucumbers, cubed
- 1 red onion, diced
- 1 green bell pepper, diced
- 1 stalk celery, diced
- 1 tablespoon sea salt
- 1 teaspoon ground black pepper
- ½ (8 ounce) bottle zesty Italian-style salad dressing

DIRECTIONS

Step 1

Combine cucumbers, red onion, bell pepper, and celery in a large bowl; season with sea salt and black pepper. Pour dressing over cucumber mixture.

Step 2

Cover bowl with plastic wrap and refrigerate at least 1 hour.

Nutrition Facts

115.3 calories; protein 1.4g 3% DV; carbohydrates 11.1g 4% DV; fat 8.1g 12% DV; cholesterolmg; sodium 1789.5mg 72% DV.

ITALIAN MEAT SAUCE II

Prep: 45 mins - **Cook:** 1 hr 30 mins - **Total:** 2 hrs 15 mins - **Servings:** 10

INGREDIENTS

- 4 tablespoons extra virgin olive oil, divided
- 1 white onion, diced
- 3 cloves garlic, crushed
- 2 (28 ounce) cans crushed tomatoes
- 2 (28 ounce) cans whole peeled tomatoes
- ¾ cup chopped Italian flat leaf parsley, divided
- 2 teaspoons garlic powder, divided
- 1 pound ground beef chuck
- 1 cup bread crumbs
- 1 egg
- 3 tablespoons milk

- salt and pepper to taste
- ½ pound hot Italian sausage
- ½ pound mild Italian sausage
- ½ pound pork neck bones
- ¼ cup red wine

DIRECTIONS

Step 1

Heat 2 tablespoons olive oil in a large saucepan over medium heat. Saute onion and garlic until onion is soft and translucent. Pour in crushed tomatoes and whole tomatoes. As you are adding the whole tomatoes, let them slowly slide through your fingers and crush them coarsely on the way into the pot. Season with 1/4 cup of the parsley and 1 teaspoon garlic powder. Cover, and reduce heat to low.

Step 2

In a large bowl, mix the ground beef chuck, breadcrumbs, 1 teaspoon garlic powder, 1/8 cup parsley, egg, milk, and salt and pepper to taste. Mix ingredients with your hands until well blended. Form into small, golf ball-size meatballs. Slice all of the sausage links but one hot and one mild link into 1/2 inch chunks.

Step 3

Heat 2 tablespoons in a large skillet over medium heat. The oil should be slightly smoking. Slice open the remaining links of hot and mild sausage, and crumble into the pan. Saute, continually breaking up the pieces, until they are all golden brown. Transfer to the sauce. Brown the meatballs, chopped sausage links, and pork bones on all sides until they are a deep golden brown. You may need to do this in stages, and continually transfer into the sauce when browned. Drain excess fat.

Step 4

Pour the red wine into the skillet and deglaze all of the brown chunks on the bottom of the pan. Let the wine reduce to about half, then transfer into the sauce. Frequently stir, and season with salt and pepper to taste for about another hour after the last meat has been transferred into the pan. Finish by stirring the remaining fresh parsley into the sauce. Spoon sauce over your favorite pasta and serve the meat on a separate plate.

Note

If you prefer not to use wine, you may substitute tomato juice or water.

Nutrition Facts

502.8 calories; protein 27.2g 54% DV; carbohydrates 28.2g 9% DV; fat 31.8g 49% DV; cholesterol 104.1mg 35% DV; sodium 1036.6mg 42% DV.

BEEFY ITALIAN RAMEN SKILLET

Prep: 10 mins **- Cook:** 15 mins **- Total:** 25 mins **- Servings:** 5

INGREDIENTS

- 1 pound ground beef, or to taste

- 16 slices pepperoni, or to taste
- 1 (14.5 ounce) can diced tomatoes
- 1 cup water
- 2 (3 ounce) packages beef-flavored ramen noodles
- 1 green bell peppers, cut into strips
- 1 cup shredded mozzarella cheese

DIRECTIONS

Step 1

Heat a large skillet over medium-high heat. Cook and stir beef and pepperoni slices in the hot skillet until beef is completely browned, 5 to 7 minutes. Stir tomatoes, water, and the seasoning packet contents from the ramen noodles into the beef mixture.

Step 2

Break ramen noodle blocks into halves and add to beef mixture with the green bell pepper; cook until the noodles soften, about 5 minutes.

Step 3

Remove skillet from heat, sprinkle mozzarella cheese over the beef mixture, and place a cover on the skillet; let mixture sit until cheese melts, 2 to 3 minutes.

Cook's Note:

This is also good with Oriental-flavor ramen.

Nutrition Facts

297.4 calories; protein 23.6g 47% DV; carbohydrates 7.4g 2% DV; fat 18.4g 28% DV; cholesterol 78mg 26% DV; sodium 546.3mg 22% DV.

BAKED ITALIAN LEMON CHICKEN

Prep: 20 mins - **Cook:** 25 mins - **Total:** 45 mins - **Servings:** 4

INGREDIENTS

- 1 serving cooking spray
- 5 tablespoons butter, melted
- 2 tablespoons lemon juice
- 1 (.7 ounce) package dry Italian salad dressing mix (such as Good Seasons®)
- 1 cup panko bread crumbs
- 1 tablespoon garlic salt
- 1 teaspoon lemon pepper
- 4 (4 ounce) skinless, boneless chicken breast halves, thinly sliced

DIRECTIONS

Step 1

Preheat oven to 375 degrees F (190 degrees C). Spray a 9x13-inch baking dish with cooking spray.

Step 2

Mix butter, lemon juice, and half the Italian dressing mix in a shallow dish until well-blended. Pour remaining Italian dressing mix in another shallow bowl and add bread crumbs, garlic salt, and lemon pepper; stir to combine.

Step 3

Dip sliced chicken into butter mixture and press into bread crumb mixture. Gently toss between your hands so any bread crumbs that haven't stuck can fall away. Arrange chicken in prepared baking sheet. Drizzle any remaining butter mixture over breaded chicken.

Step 4

Bake in preheated oven until chicken is no longer pink in the center and juices run clean, 25 to 30 minutes.

Cook's Note:

I just found a product called True Lemon crystallized lemon. Add a few packets to the bread crumbs to taste if you want a bit more lemon flavor.

Editor's Note:

The nutrition data for this recipe includes the full amount of the breading ingredients. The actual amount of the breading consumed will vary.

Nutrition Facts

338.1 calories; protein 26.7g 53% DV; carbohydrates 22.4g 7% DV; fat 18g 28% DV; cholesterol 102.8mg 34% DV; sodium 2561.2mg 102% DV.

ITALIAN TUNA SPREAD

Prep: 15 mins - **Total:** 15 mins - **Servings:** 8

INGREDIENTS

- 3 (4.5 ounce) cans tuna packed in olive oil, drained
- ½ cup unsalted butter at room temperature
- 3 tablespoons capers, drained
- 1 tablespoon chopped Italian flat-leaf parsley
- 1 teaspoon lemon juice
- 1 pinch salt and ground black pepper to taste

DIRECTIONS

Step 1

Blend tuna, butter, capers, parsley, lemon juice, salt, and pepper in a food processor until smooth.

Nutrition Facts

158.4 calories; protein 12.4g 25% DV; carbohydrates 0.3g; fat 11.9g 18% DV; cholesterol 44.9mg 15% DV;

sodium 121.4mg 5% DV.

PROSCIUTTO E MELONE (ITALIAN HAM AND MELON)

Prep: 10 mins - **Total:** 10 mins - **Servings:** 4

INGREDIENTS

- 1 cantaloupe - seeded and cut into 8 wedges
- 8 thin slices prosciutto

DIRECTIONS

Step 1

Remove the flesh from the rind of the cantaloupe; wrap each piece of cantaloupe with a slice of the ham. Serve cold.

Nutrition Facts

99.3 calories; protein 3.9g 8% DV; carbohydrates 11.3g 4% DV; fat 4.8g 7% DV; cholesterol 12.5mg 4% DV; sodium 296.4mg 12% DV.

GRILLED ITALIAN PORK CHOPS

Prep: 10 mins - **Cook:** 10 mins **Additional:** 5 mins - **Total:** 25 mins - **Servings:** 4

INGREDIENTS

- 4 eaches (3/4 inch thick) pork chops
- 1 pinch salt and ground black pepper to taste
- 4 slices ham
- 4 slices tomato
- 4 slices mozzarella cheese
- 1 teaspoon chopped fresh oregano to taste
- 1 pinch paprika to taste

DIRECTIONS

Step 1

Preheat an outdoor grill for medium heat, and lightly oil the grate.

Step 2

Sprinkle pork chops with salt and black pepper, and grill until the chops are browned, show good grill marks, and are no longer pink in the middle, 5 to 8 minutes per side. An instant-read meat thermometer inserted into the center of a chop should read at least 145 degrees F (63 degrees C).

Step 3

Place ham, tomato, and mozzarella cheese slices on each pork chop, and sprinkle with oregano and paprika; cook until the cheese has melted, about 2 more minutes. Let stand for 5 minutes before serving.

Nutrition Facts

378.7 calories; protein 52.5g 105% DV; carbohydrates 3.1g 1% DV; fat 16g 25% DV; cholesterol 140.4mg 47% DV; sodium 606.5mg 24% DV.

ITALIAN MINI MEAT LOAVES

Prep: 10 mins - **Cook:** 45 mins - **Total:** 55 mins - **Servings:** 4

INGREDIENTS

- 2 tablespoons olive oil
- 1 pound lean ground beef
- 8 ounces bulk mild Italian sausage
- ½ cup diced white onion
- 1 (24 ounce) jar Classico® Fresh Four Cheese Sauce, divided
- 1 egg, lightly beaten
- ⅓ cup Italian seasoned bread crumbs
- ¼ cup shredded Parmesan cheese
- ¼ teaspoon garlic powder
- ½ teaspoon salt
- ⅛ teaspoon black pepper
- 1 tablespoon chopped fresh parsley
- 1 cup shredded mozzarella cheese

DIRECTIONS

Step 1

Heat oven to 350 degrees F. Generously oil the bottom of a 9x13-inch baking dish.

Step 2

Mix together the ground beef and Italian sausage in a large bowl. Add onion, half of the jar of four-cheese red sauce, egg, bread crumbs, Parmesan cheese, garlic powder, salt, pepper, and parsley. Mix until well blended.

Step 3

Divide mixture into 4 oval mini loaves; place in prepared baking dish. Pour the remaining red sauce over tops of meat loaves.

Step 4

Spray the underside of a large piece of foil with nonstick cooking spray; cover dish tightly.

Step 5

Bake for 45 minutes. Uncover and sprinkle loaves with shredded mozzarella cheese.

Step 6

Increase the oven temperature to 400 degrees F. Bake uncovered until cheese is melted and the internal temperature reaches 165 degrees F, about 10 more minutes.

Nutrition Facts

674.6 calories; protein 43.6g 87% DV; carbohydrates 27.8g 9% DV; fat 42.9g 66% DV; cholesterol 172.1mg 57% DV; sodium 1862.7mg 75% DV.

ITALIAN MEAT AND SPINACH PIE

Prep: 45 mins - **Cook:** 1 hr 20 mins **Additional:** 10 mins - **Total:** 2 hrs 15 mins - **Servings:** 8

INGREDIENTS

- 1 recipe pastry for a 9-inch pie crust
- ½ pound ground beef
- ½ pound mild or hot turkey Italian sausage, casings removed
- 1 clove garlic, minced
- 1 onion, chopped
- ¾ cup chopped red bell pepper
- 10 ounces sliced fresh mushrooms
- 1 clove garlic, minced
- 1 (6 ounce) can tomato paste
- 1 ¼ cups water
- ½ teaspoon salt
- 1 teaspoon dried basil
- ½ teaspoon dried oregano
- 1 (10 ounce) package frozen chopped spinach, thawed and well drained
- 1 cup part-skim ricotta cheese
- 1 ½ cups shredded mozzarella cheese, divided
- 1 cup chopped, seeded plum tomatoes
- 1 (6 ounce) can sliced black olives, drained

DIRECTIONS

Step 1

Line a 9-inch pie pan with the pastry and press the edges of the crust with a fork to seal it to the pie dish. Cover loosely with plastic wrap and refrigerate while you prepare the sauce.

Step 2

Heat a large skillet over medium-high heat and stir in the ground beef, turkey sausage, and 1 clove of minced garlic. Cook and stir until the meat is crumbly, evenly browned, and no longer pink. Drain and discard any excess grease. Add the onion, red bell pepper, and mushrooms and cook, stirring frequently, until the onion is soft and translucent and the mushrooms have given off their liquid, about 5 minutes. Add the remaining garlic and cook for 30 seconds.

Step 3

Stir in the tomato paste, water, salt, basil, and oregano and bring the sauce to a boil. Reduce the heat to low, cover, and simmer for 10 minutes. Remove from heat and set aside.

Step 4

Preheat an oven to 450 degrees F (230 degrees C).

Step 5

Line the chilled pie crust with a double thickness of aluminum foil. Bake for 9 minutes. Remove the foil and continue baking until the bottom of the crust is set, about 7 more minutes (see Editor's Note for tips). Remove from the oven and set aside. Reduce the oven temperature to 350 degrees F (175 degrees C).

Step 6

Combine the spinach, ricotta, and 1/2 cup mozzarella cheese. Spoon the filling into the baked crust. Top with the meat mixture. Cover the edges of the pie crust with foil to prevent over-browning, place the pie on a baking sheet, and bake for 45 minutes.

Step 7

Remove the pie from the oven. Top the meat mixture with 1 cup of mozzarella cheese, chopped tomatoes, and sliced olives. Return it to the oven and bake until the cheese is melted, about 10 minutes. Let stand for 10 minutes before serving.

Editor's Notes

This pie can be made ahead of time. Bake it as directed, allow it to cool, and then wrap well with aluminum foil and freeze for up to 2 months. Reheat the pie in a 350 degrees F (175 degrees C) oven, still wrapped in foil, until heated through, about 45 minutes. Remove foil and bake until cheese is bubbling, 10 to 15 minutes more.

Nutrition Facts

398.3 calories; protein 24.7g 49% DV; carbohydrates 25.4g 8% DV; fat 22.9g 35% DV; cholesterol 60.1mg 20% DV; sodium 1098.4mg 44% DV.

ITALIAN SAUSAGE PENNE

Prep: 15 mins - **Cook:** 15 mins - **Total:** 30 mins - **Servings:** 6

INGREDIENTS

- 1 (16 ounce) package penne pasta
- 1 (19 ounce) package Johnsonville® Mild Italian Sausage Links, coin-sliced
- 1 tablespoon olive oil
- 1 medium green bell pepper, julienned

- 1 medium red bell pepper, julienned
- 1 medium onion, halved and sliced
- 1 clove garlic, minced
- 1 (28 ounce) jar marinara sauce, heated

DIRECTIONS

Step 1

Cook pasta according to package directions.

Step 2

In skillet, brown sausage in oil for 3-4 minutes. Add peppers, onion and garlic. Continue to cook until vegetables are tender.

Step 3

Divide prepared pasta in bowls, top with marinara sauce and sausage vegetable mixture.

Nutrition Facts

725.6 calories; protein 27.6g 55% DV; carbohydrates 77.4g 25% DV; fat 34g 52% DV; cholesterol 71.3mg 24% DV; sodium 1386.8mg 56% DV.

ITALIAN LEMON CREAM CAKE

Prep: 20 mins - **Cook:** 30 mins Additional: 4 hrs - **Total:** 4 hrs 50 mins - **Servings:** 12

INGREDIENTS

- 1 serving Cooking spray
- 1 (16.25 ounce) package white cake mix
- ¾ cup milk
- 1 tablespoon milk
- 2 large eggs eggs
- 3 ½ tablespoons vegetable oil
- Crumb Topping:
- 2 tablespoons butter, melted
- ½ teaspoon vanilla extract
- 4 ounces cream cheese, softened
- ⅔ cup confectioners' sugar, divided, plus more for dusting
- 3 tablespoons lemon juice
- 1 teaspoon grated lemon zest
- 2 cups heavy whipping cream

DIRECTIONS

Step 1

Preheat oven to 350 degrees F (175 degrees C). Spray the bottom of a 10-inch springform pan with Cooking spray.

Step 2

Measure 1 cup cake mix; set aside for crumb topping. Place the remaining cake mix in a large bowl; add 3/4 cup plus 1 tablespoon milk, eggs, and oil. Beat cake mix mixture using an electric mixer until batter is thoroughly combined, about 2 minutes. Pour batter into the prepared pan.

Step 3

Mix melted butter and vanilla extract together in a bowl; stir in reserved 1 cup cake mix until mixture is crumbly. Sprinkle crumbs over top of cake batter.

Step 4

Bake in the preheated oven until a toothpick inserted in the center of the cake comes out clean, 30 to 35 minutes. Cool cake to room temperature in the pan.

Step 5

Beat cream cheese, 1/3 cup confectioners' sugar, lemon juice, and lemon zest together in a bowl until smooth and creamy. Beat cream and remaining 1/3 cup confectioners' sugar together in a separate bowl using an electric mixer until stiff peaks form. Fold cream cheese mixture into whipped cream.

Step 6

Remove cake from springform pan. Cut cake horizontally into 2 layers using a serrated knife; remove top layer. Spread filling onto the bottom cake layer; place top cake over filling. Refrigerate cake for at least 4 hours. Dust cake with more confectioners' sugar before serving.

Nutrition Facts

434.5 calories; protein 4.9g 10% DV; carbohydrates 39.5g 13% DV; fat 29.2g 45% DV; cholesterol 102.1mg 34% DV; sodium 330.2mg 13% DV.

ITALIAN LASAGNA

Servings: 15

INGREDIENTS

- 9 thick slices bacon, diced
- 1 onion, chopped
- 1 teaspoon fennel seed
- 1 teaspoon dried oregano
- 1 ½ teaspoons Italian seasoning
- 2 (28 ounce) cans tomato sauce
- 2 pounds Italian sausage
- 1 (16 ounce) package lasagna noodles
- 2 pints part-skim ricotta cheese

- 2 large eggs eggs
- 2 teaspoons chopped fresh parsley
- 1 teaspoon dried oregano
- ⅓ cup milk
- 8 slices provolone cheese
- 6 cups shredded mozzarella cheese

DIRECTIONS

Step 1

Brown bacon and onion in a large pan over medium heat. Stir in fennel seed, 1 teaspoon oregano, Italian seasoning, and tomato sauce. Cover, and simmer on low for 4 to 6 hours, or until thick.

Step 2

Brown sausage links in a large skillet. Drain on paper towels. Cut into 1 inch pieces.

Step 3

Mix together ricotta cheese, egg, milk, parsley, and 1 teaspoon oregano in a medium bowl.

Step 4

Layer 1 cup of sauce on the bottom of a 9 x 13 inch pan. Layer with 1/3 unCooked lasagna noodles, 1/2 ricotta cheese mixture, 1/2 sausage pieces, 1/3 mozzarella, and 1/2 provolone cheese. Top with 1/3 sauce. Repeat layers. Top with remaining 1/3 noodles. Spread remaining sauce over the top, and sprinkle with remaining 1/3 mozzarella cheese.

Step 5

Bake at 350 degrees F (175 degrees C) for 1 1/2 hours.

Nutrition Facts

754.8 calories; protein 40.2g 80% DV; carbohydrates 34.4g 11% DV; fat 51g 78% DV; cholesterol 156.1mg 52% DV; sodium 1701.9mg 68% DV.

Printed in Great Britain
by Amazon